Religion and Rationality

Books by Jürgen Habermas included in the series
Studies in Contemporary German Social Thought
Thomas McCarthy, general editor

Religion and Rationality

Essays on Reason, God, and Modernity

Jürgen Habermas

edited and with an introduction by
Eduardo Mendieta

The MIT Press

Cambridge, Massachusetts

First MIT Press edition, 2002

© 2002 Polity Press

Printed and bound in Great Britain by TJ International, Padstow, Cornwall.

Library of Congress Control Number: 2002101841

ISBN 0-262-08312-4 (hardcover)
      0-262-58216-3 (paperback)

This book is printed on acid-free paper.

Contents

Acknowledgments

This collection of Habermas' essays on religion has not previously appeared in one volume. The Introduction and chapter 8 (translated by Max Pensky) have been written especially for this volume. Full bibliographical details of the other chapters are given below. Each chapter in this volume has been presented as it was originally published. The decision to do this has necessarily entailed some inconsistencies of style and spelling between the chapters.

Chapter 1, "The German Idealism of the Jewish Philosophers," first appeared as "Der deutsche Idealismus der jüdischen Philosophen," in *Philosophisch-politische Profile Erweiterte Ausgabe*, pp. 39–64, © Suhrkamp Verlag, 1981. It was translated by Frederick G. Lawrence and published in English as *Philosophical-Political Profiles* (MIT, 1983 and Polity, 1986), pp. 21–43, © MIT, 1983.

Chapter 2, "On the Difficulty of Saying No," first appeared as "Von der Schwierigkeit, Nein zu sagen," in *Philosophisch-politische Profile. Erweiterte Ausgabe*, pp. 445–52, © Suhrkamp Verlag, 1981. This is a new translation by Max Pensky (© Polity, 2002).

Chapter 3, "Transcendence from Within, Transcendence in this World," first appeared as "Transzendenz von innen, Transzendenz ins Diesseits," in *Texte und Kontexte*, pp. 127–56, © Suhrkamp Verlag, 1991. It was translated by Eric Crump and Peter P. Kenny and was published in Don S. Browning and Francis Schüssler Fiorenza, eds., *Habermas, Modernity, and Public Theology*, Crossroad, 1992, pp. 226–50, © Don S. Browning and Francis Schüssler Fiorenza.

Chapter 4, "To Seek to Salvage an Unconditional Meaning Without God is a Futile Undertaking," first appeared as "Zu Max Horkheimers

Satz: Einen unbedingten Sinn zu retten ohne Gott ist eitel," in *Texte und Kontexte*, pp. 110–26, © Suhrkamp Verlag 1991. It was translated by Ciaran P. Cronin and published in *Justification and Application. Remarks on Discourse Ethics* (MIT and Polity, 1993), pp. 133–46, © MIT Press, 1993.

Chapters 5 and 6, "Communicative Freedom and Negative Theology" and "Israel or Athens: Where does Anamnestic Reason belong?" appeared as "Kommunikative Freiheit und Negative Theologie" and "Israel oder Athen: Wem gehört die anamnetische Vernunft?" in *Vom sinnlichen Eindruck zum symbolischen Ausdruck Philosophische Essays*, pp. 112–35 and 98–111 respectively, © Suhrkamp Verlag, 1997. They were translated by Peter Dews and published in *The Liberating Power of Symbols. Philosophical Essays*, pp. 90–111 and 78–89 respectively, © Polity.

Chapter 7, "Tracing the Other of History in History. Gershom Scholem's *Sabbati Sevi*," first appeared as "In der Geschichte das Andere der Geschichte aufspüren. Zu Gershom Scholems *Sabbatai Zwi*," in *Vom sinnlichen Eindruck zum symbolischen Ausdruck Philosophische Essays*, pp. 73–83, © Suhrkamp Verlag, 1997. It was translated by Peter Dews and published in *The Liberating Power of Symbols. Philosophical Essays* (MIT and Polity, 2001), pp. 57–65, © Polity, 2001.

Every effort has been made to trace the copyright holders, but if any has been inadvertently overlooked, the publishers will be pleased to make the necessary arrangements at the first opportunity.

Introduction

The question of religion is once again at the forefront of critical
thought precisely because it crystallizes some of the most serious
and pressing questions of contemporary social thought: the relationship between social structure and rationality; between reason as a
universal standard and the inescapable fact that reason is embodied
only historically and in contingent social practices; that reason
as universality was, if not discovered, at least enunciated as a teleological standard by religions;[1] that in an age of secularization and sci-
enticization, religion remains a major factor in the moral education
and motivation of individuals uprooted from other traditions; and at
the very least, in an age of accelerating homogenization and simultaneous manufacturing of difference, what sociologists of globalization have called *glocalization*, religions are articulated as the last
refuge of unadulterated difference, the last reservoir of cultural
autonomy.

Jürgen Habermas' work over the last four decades intersects sometimes directly and explicitly, sometimes tangentially and suggestively,
with many of these questions. The impetus is to make explicit what
to many is implicit and unthematized. The goal, thus, is to foreground
those resources in Habermas' immense intellectual contribution that
may aid a critical confrontation with the new intellectual and social
challenges that are entailed by new forms of obscurantism, fundamentalism, anarchical mysticism, religious irrationalism, and the like.
Most importantly, this collection should make evident how those
resources in Habermas' work were forged from the very sources and
traditions that have shaped the identity and structure of Western

societies. Habermas' "methodological atheism" is not a rejection but a response to and a dialectical sublation of the Jewish-Christian tradition that suffuses so pervasively the work of all of his precursors.

Another goal of this collection is to make explicit, if the question was ever posed, how Habermas' work inherited, appropriating and transforming it, the critical tradition of Jewish utopian messianism of the early Frankfurt School. In what follows, therefore, I turn to a brief and broad characterization of this Jewish messianic utopianism. I then proceed to reconstruct the main elements and strains of Habermas' treatment of religion. The central thesis of this later section is that Habermas' treatment is not correctly characterized by the image of a temporal rupture between an early positive and a later negative appraisal of the role of religion. Instead, textual evidence will be elicited that suggests an ever present appreciation of religion that fluctuates with the angle of approach, or lens of analysis. In other words, it will be suggested that Habermas' statements, whether positive or negative, are determined by whether he is broaching the question from a philosophical and critical perspective, or from a sociological, political, and legal perspective.

Religion as Critique

Albert Schweitzer began his classic work, *The Quest of the Historical Jesus*, with the statement, "When, at some future day, our period of civilization shall lie, closed and completed, before the eyes of later generations, German theology will stand out as a great, a unique phenomenon in the mental and spiritual life of our time."[2] He wrote this shortly after the turn of the century, in 1906. In parallel, today, as we look back over the century of extremes, as Hobsbawm called the twentieth century, we may claim that Jewish thought will stand out as a unique social and intellectual phenomenon. The secular, apocalyptic, utopian and pessimistic messianism of the Jewish thinkers of the generation of 1914 crystallized some of the most painful lessons of the age of mass extermination and mass culture. After Auschwitz, as Adorno put it, "[a] new categorical imperative has been imposed by Hitler upon unfree mankind: to arrange their thoughts and actions so that Auschwitz will not repeat itself, so that nothing similar will happen."[3]

Nonetheless, following Michael Löwy, we should seek to be less evocative and more precise.[4] It was the Central European Jews who were able to achieve the most creative and lasting synthesis and transformation, of both Judaism and Christianity, in the twentieth century. But we would have to go beyond Löwy, and suggest that the height of this creative upsurge was best embodied in the work of the first generation of the Frankfurt School, in the work of Max Horkheimer, Theodor W. Adorno, Walter Benjamin, Herbert Marcuse, and Erich Fromm and Leo Lowenthal, to extend legitimately Gershom Scholem's list.[5] Their work, it should be noted, was deeply influenced and guided by the work of Ernst Bloch, Georg Lukács, and also Franz Rosenzweig and Martin Buber.[6]

This creative furor during the first decades of the twentieth century, which has been called the Jewish generation of 1914, in Germany in particular, and in Frankfurt and Berlin even more specifically, could be analyzed sociologically.[7] Jewish assimilation had reached its zenith in Germany at the very moment when industrialization, urbanization, and secularization had reach their most extreme levels of acceleration. The German-Jewish question had found its answer in the dissolution of the Jewish into the German without residue or trace. Simultaneously, a young generation of secular and assimilated Jewish intellectuals began to discover and make explicit this one-sided assimilation. They found themselves to be both pariahs and unwanted, marginalized and excluded, as Jews. Despite their confession of Germanness, they remained suspect: once a Jew, always a Jew. Assimilation is unmasked as a pyrrhic victory, as an asymmetrical and non-reciprocal immersion into a polis and culture that still resents their identity, as dispossession and abandonment of a tradition that at least offered a cultural and moral compass. At this very moment, the promise of modernity turns into a malaise: alienation, reification, rootlessness, superficiality, crassness, qualitative leveling for the sake of quantitative maximization, i.e. massification, and so on. It is thus that a romantic critique of capitalism, and modern society in general, begins to be enunciated. This anti-capitalist romanticism, to use Lukács' apt expression, does not fit the traditional taxonomy of responses to modernization: left, centrist, or conservative. It is not easy to associate a particular political attitude with a particular philosophical and epistemological perspective. Elements of so-called conservative ontology and metaphysics are deployed with the intent of enunciating a radical and leftist critique of capitalism. Mostly committed to the values of the Enlightenment, which had catalyzed their incomplete assimilation, and set adrift from their traditions by centuries of secularization, de-assimilation, and religious amnesia,[8] Jewish intellectuals were poised in a unique social position from which they could seek to salvage and refashion their religious traditions while at the same time trying to save the best of the Enlightenment from the corrosive effects of capitalism. It was out of this dialectical tension that a unique type of Jewish messianism was articulated by Central European Jews, and Frankfurt assimilated Jews in particular.[9]

Philosophically, and conceptually, the Jewish messianism of these Central European and German Jews could be said to be composed of four elements, always present with varying degrees of emphasis in different thinkers. Following Anson Rabinbach, we can differentiate them in the following way. First, this Jewish messianism is profoundly characterized by a restorative element. This has to do with anamnesis as a fundamental aspect of rationality. In contrast to the idea of the restitution of an Arcadian past, or golden age, this messianism seeks to restore by way of an apocalyptic re-enactment. Second, this messianism is utopian in that it projects a new age that is not brought about by the progressive accumulation of improvements, through a quantitative meliorism. This utopianism is unlike Enlightenment utopianism, which sees the future as the mere actualization of the present. Instead, the truly utopian is to be seen as an irruption into the historical continuum by a trans-historical agent. With Benjamin, we may say that progress is catastrophe, and utopia is ahistorical. The third element, already alluded to, is the apocalyptic dimension of this messianism. The restoration of wholeness, *Tikkun*, and the irruption of utopia, two aspects of one and the same process, are only conceivable as a radical discontinuity with the present. The past, as the past of injustice, is not to be superficially reconciled in the present, and the future is not imaginable from the present, lest it become a mere mirror image of what that present can alone think and project. Radical reconciliation and utopia are only possible on the assumption of temporal discontinuity. Fourth, and finally, the restorative, utopian, and apocalyptic elements converge in the ambivalent image of messianism. This messianism, most importantly, is not personalizable. It is not the waiting or announcement of a messiah, but the call and discernment of the messianic forces and elements that, like fragments of utopia, break into the continuum of history. To this extent, this messianism is a priori undecidable, indeterminate. In other words, this messianism, which rejects the present and the possibility of meliorative progress, is ambiguously pessimistic and passive, but also wildly expectant and vigilant. Expectation, readiness, wakefulness, but also profound passivity, humility, and patience – these are the extremes between which the Jewish messianism of these turn-of-the-century Jewish pariahs wavered.[10]

A careful reading of the work produced by the members of the Institute for Social Research, as well as the people attached to it, reveal a sustained and in-depth concern with questions of religion, theology, the sociology of religion, theological metaphysics, and the history of religious ideas.[11] Max Horkheimer himself contributed a series of essays in which the theme of religion is substantive if not central.[12] Yet it must also be acknowledged that a study of the particular critique of religion developed by the first generation of the Frankfurt School has remained unexecuted, because of the trans-disciplinary, or adisciplinary, character of such a critique.[13] In other words, the work of the early Frankfurt School on religion has remained elusive because of the difficulty of placing it within the traditional disciplinary boundaries we associate with the study of religion. Their work did not fall within the category of the study of religions, sociology of religion, or even philosophy of religion. Nor could it have been assimilated to theology, notwithstanding repeated accusations that Critical Theory was really masked theology.[14] What makes the contributions of members of the early Frankfurt School, like the early Fromm, Marcuse, even Lowenthal, Horkheimer, and Adorno, so unique is precisely the way they developed a *sui generis* approach to the question of religion. For them, the issue of religion had to be approached philosophically, historically, sociologically, psychologically, even from the standpoint of metaphysics and ontology. The point, in fact, was to rescue from theology and religion that which is in danger of being extinguished and desecrated by their attempt to render positive that which can only be ciphered negatively.[15] As Horkheimer put it in a letter that became the foreword to Martin Jay's history of the Frankfurt School, "The appeal to an entirely other [*ein ganz Anderes*] than this world had primarily a social-philosophical impetus. It led finally to a more positive evaluation of certain metaphysical trends, because the empirical 'whole is the untrue' (Adorno). The hope that earthly horror does not possess the last word is, to be sure, a non-scientific wish."[16]

In order to further characterize the unique aspects of this critique of religion, and given our purposes in this introduction, it should suffice to focus on Max Horkheimer's and Theodor Adorno's relationship to the previously demarcated Jewish messianism. Evidently, in their religious atheistic, to use an expression of Lukács,[17] or non-secular secularist, to use an expression of Scholem,[18] response to their Jewishness and the challenges of modernity, as well as to the crisis of Marxism in the early decades of the twentieth century, we find developed and summarized the critiques of religion which are exhibited in their two most extreme forms in the works of the key figures of Ernst Bloch and, of course, Walter Benjamin. The former stands for the utopian and forward-looking while the latter stands for the redemptive and anamnestic. Although both remained institutionally peripheral to the Frankfurt School and the Institute for Social Research, they remained central to the intellectual constellation that configured that unique cultural phenomenon called Frankfurt School Critical Theory.[19]

It must be made clear from the outset that Max Horkheimer's work was marked by a continued and unwavering interest in religion.[20] From his earliest aphorisms, to his last writings, interviews, and obituaries, there is an ever present confrontation, treatment, and concern with the question of the role of religion in contemporary societies.[21] The best-known example of this preoccupation with the so-called demise of religion, i.e. the secularization thesis, is to be found in Horkheimer's essay written for a *Festschrift* for Adorno, "Theism and Atheism." In this essay we find the statement which became the focus as well as the title of one of the essays by Habermas included in this book. The statement reads:

> Without God one will try in vain to preserve absolute meaning. No matter how independent a given form of expression may be within its own sphere as in art or religion, and no matter how distinct and how necessary in itself, with the belief in God it will have to surrender all to being objectively something higher than a practical convenience ... The death of God is also the death of eternal truth.[22]

The other statement comes from an interview Horkheimer granted in 1967 on the occasion of Paul Tillich's death: "I believe that there is no philosophy to which I could assent which did not contain a theological moment, for it relates indeed to the recognition of how much the world in which we live is to be interpreted as relative."[23] Evidently, there are numerous analogous statements. A wonderful collection of aphorisms by Horkheimer on the need for the totally other, the entirely other, as a social, anthropological, and even metaphysical need could be easily edited.[24]

These, and many, many more assertions, however, are marked by two central motifs. First, that religion retains an ineradicable philosophical and conceptual importance, without which criticism of actuality and society is unthinkable. And, second, that insofar as religion means belief in an absolutely transcendent God who hovers above history as ultimate judge, then the promise of justice and hope that is not exhausted by any social institution is kept alive. Indeed, as he suggests at the end of his essay "Theism and Atheism," our relationship to religion remains an index of resistance. In times of atheism and the glorification of terrestrial powers, theism becomes an act of defiance and nonconformism, of not going along with the powers that be. In times of theism, when again the powers that be are legitimated with reference to some projection of the divine, atheism becomes an act of resistance, precisely in the name of that which must always remain unrepresented. The Jewish ban on the representation, even in writing, of the holy one is in Horkheimer's view not only a theologumenon, but even a fundamental concept of the dialectic. That we cannot say anything absolutely about God is assimilated into one of Critical Theory's foundational presuppositions: that the absolute is unrepresentable.[25] In Adorno's words, it is not that we have the identity of the identical and the non-identical, but the non-identity of the identical and the non-identical. A thought that would claim to present the totality as representable in any form whatsoever would have already succumbed to the logic of identity thinking. But, as Horkheimer notes, the rejection of the possibility of the representation of the absolute is to be preserved for the sake of the individual, the singular, that which has suffered the ignominy of a history that has been lived hitherto as catastrophe. In Horkheimer's work, then, the yearning for a wholly other is a figure of thought that seeks to preserve the "longing that unites all men so that the horrible events, the injustice of history so far would not be permitted to the final, ultimate fate of the victims."[26]

In Adorno's case, his work is so permeated by the apocalyptic, utopian, Jewish messianism that some have thrown at it the accusation that it is no more than negative theology, a form of medieval mystical irrationalism.[27] Here what Benjamin says about his work's relationship to theology might also be said of Adorno's parallel relationship to theology: "My thinking is related to theology as a blotting pad is related to ink. It is saturated with it. Were one to go by the blotter, however, nothing of what is written would remain."[28] Indeed, as Adorno himself wrote to Benjamin in 1935, "A restoration of theology, or better still, a radicalization dialectic introduced into the glowing heart of theology, would simultaneously require the utmost intensification of the social-dialectical, and indeed, economic motifs."[29] It is in the light of this double, dialectical strategy that we must read Adorno's critique of religion.

One may venture the assertion that Adorno's works are not just an attempt to do exactly what he calls us to do at the end of *Minima Moralia*, namely to think from the standpoint of redemption, but further, to exalt the theological content of thought to its extreme. But to do so means to do it negatively: Preservation by negation, refusing to accept the assimilation of the singular into the concept, without relinquishing the means of the concept. The other, as the irreplaceable and unrepresentable singularity, can only be referred to indirectly and through the deciphering of the traces of violence inflicted on the other, the individual, by the concept itself. This is why negative dialectics is a synthesis of a phenomenology of existence that grants us the view from immanence with the dialectics of concepts that traces their genesis by way of determinate negation: how they emerged from a specific societal context. This means, specifically with reference to religion, that that which dwells in the religious can only be rescued and transmitted by way of the critique of the concepts and theologumenon in which it has been preserved. As he put it in his essay "Reason and Revelation": "If religion is accepted for the sake of something other than its own truth content, then it undermines itself."[30] In Adorno's view, we can no more unhinge critical thought from metaphysics, albeit transformed, than we can uncouple metaphysics from theology.[31]

Adorno, like Benjamin and Bloch, practiced the art of philosophizing by way of apothegms, verbal diamonds of refracted wisdom. Here, however, I will not succumb to the temptation to concatenate citation after citation. I will merely gloss over a few.[32] In *Negative Dialectics*, for instance, he writes:

Anyone who would nail down transcendence can rightly be charged –
as by Karl Kraus, for instance – with lack of imagination, anti-
intellectualism, and thus a betrayal of transcendence. On the other
hand, if the possibility, however feeble and distant, of redemption
in existence is cut off altogether, the human spirit would become an
illusion, and the finite, conditioned, merely existing subject would
eventually be deified as carrier of the spirit.[33]

Transcendence, as the wholly other, the numinous and divine, but also
as the element of unconditionality in every human being, is neither
to be shabbily represented nor to be skeptically disposed of. Metaphysics, and theology as its precursor, had the intention of capturing
this reference to the other by way of the immanent in life and history,
while being aware that such attempts were always being put in jeop-
ardy. Thus, the critique of metaphysics is itself an instantiation of the
metaphysical impulse to point to the transcendent. As Adorno continues in the same section from the *Negative Dialectics*:

The idea of truth is supreme among the metaphysical ideas, and this
is where it takes us. It is why one who believes in God cannot believe
in God, why the possibility represented by the divine name is maintained, rather, by him who does not believe. Once upon a time the
image ban extended to pronouncing the name; now the ban itself has
in that form come to evoke suspicions of superstition. The ban has
been exacerbated: the mere thought of hope is a transgression against
it, an act of working against it.[34]

These words echo the sentences that close his already cited essay
"Reason and Revelation": "I see no other possibility than an extreme
ascesis toward any type of revealed faith, an extreme loyalty to
the prohibition of images, far beyond what this once originally
meant."[35] We must reject hope for the sake of that which it pointed
to, namely truth, but truth as the unconditional that renders
everything intramundane something relative and contingent, as
Horkheimer put it.

We have to wonder whether in fact Adorno meant to reject
hoping, *toto caelo*. After all, he had written earlier in *Minima Moralia*:
"In the end hope, wrested from reality by negating it, is the only form
in which truth appears. Without hope, the idea of truth would
be scarcely even thinkable, and it is the cardinal untruth, having

recognized existence to be bad, to present it as truth simply because it has been recognized."[36] Hope is the guarantee of truth precisely because hope unmasks the givenness of reality. Hope, the yearning after the possibility of that which would totally transform the present, renders reality incomplete and inconclusive. Truth is beyond the now. Hence, "the whole is the untrue." And if this beyond that renders the now transcendable is not to be betrayed, then hope must also be qualified. Therefore, in an alternate formulation articulated in a dialogue with Bloch, Adorno puts it this way "Falsum – the false thing – index sui et veri. [The false is the sign of itself and the true.]"[37] This aphorism, which condenses the impetus of *Negative Dialectics*, is also expressed in a provocative and paradoxical formulation enunciated later in the same dialogue: "Actually I would think that unless there is no kind of trace of truth in the ontological proof of the existence of God, that is, unless the element of its reality is also already conveyed in the power of the concept itself, there could not only be no utopia but there could also not be any thinking."[38] To which Bloch retorted:

> In hope, the matter concerns perfection, and to that extent it concerns the ontological proof of the existence of God. But the most perfect creature is posited by Anselm as something fixed that includes the most real at the same time. Such a tenet is not defensible. But what is true is that each and every criticism of imperfection, incompleteness, intolerance, and impatience already without a doubt presupposes the conception of, and longing for, a possible perfection.[39]

I think that Adorno would have answered back, as he did several times throughout the dialogue with the following words: "D'accord."

I would like to suggest that Adorno's and Horkheimer's reflections on religion can be provisionally summarized in the following way. First, enlightenment is catalyzed by religion. We cannot understand the critique of myth without understanding how religion itself, and in particular the Christian and Jewish traditions, are forms of demythologization. Second, religion, despite having accelerated the process of its own assimilation and secularization, is never divested of both its social and philosophical role: as the call to universality and the promise of an inextinguishable negativity that renders all claims to completeness and fulfillment questionable and partial. Third, while elements of criticism, or anamnesis, and utopian projecting might have migrated toward the aesthetic and the moral, religion remains both a reservoir and a compendium of humanity's most deeply felt injustices and yearned for dreams of reconciliation. Fourth, insofar as Critical Theory is a bringing together of different research tools, which ought to allow for the use of reason against reason, its approach to religion is guided by a "methodological skepticism" that ought to render one ever vigilant to facile and glib dismissals of certain social phenomena. Religion is not to be dismissed simply because a certain school of sociology has discovered, given its methodological orientation, that religion has become functionally superfluous. Fifth, and finally, the Frankfurt School's critique of religion, which is less a rejection and more a reappropriation, refuses to answer in favor of one or the other side of the dyad: Athens or Jerusalem? One is unthinkable without the other. Reason is impossible without anamnesis, and memory remains ineffective if it were not married to universality: remembrance of what and for whom? memory of suffering by whom and for whom?[40]

The Linguistification of the Sacred as a Catalyst of Modernity

While the reception of Habermas by theologians and sociologists of religion continues to gain momentum,[41] his reception by philosophers as a philosopher of religion remains incipient.[42] Philosophers and social theorists in general have taken Habermas' pronouncements on religion in his *Theory of Communicative Action*, especially in volume 2,[43] and his sporadic and pointed criticisms against mysticism and messianism in *The Philosophical Discourse of Modernity*,[44] as definitive and representative of his general outlook. It would seem, from a quick and superficial reading of passages in these two works, that Habermas has put religion to rest, and has pronounced its theoretical and social-developmental death. In fact, a consensus has developed around the notion that Habermas' theory of the "linguistification of the sacred" entails the sublimation or *Aufhebung* of religion *tout court*. This misleading representation and conclusion about Habermas' positions on religion has made it undesirable, even unnecessary, to engage him any further as an insightful philosopher of religion.[45] This is most unfortunate, for if anything, Habermas has opened up a path for a renewed dialogue with religion, whether as a source of concepts or a fundamental element in lived experience. He has neither unequivocally rejected nor half-heartedly accepted calls for a turn to religion in an age of catastrophe. The point, as he writes, is "not to overcome modernity by having recourse to archaic sources, but to take specific account of the conditions of modern postmetaphysical thought, under which an ontotheologically insulated discourse with God cannot be continued."[46] The term "postmetaphysical" here carries conceptual weight, and it is not an empty rhetorical gesture. Postmetaphysical refers to a condition not just of philosophy, but also of religion. As Habermas makes explicit:

> I do not believe that we, as Europeans, can seriously understand concepts like morality and ethical life, persons and individuality, or freedom and emancipation, without appropriating the substance of the Judeo-Christian understanding of history in terms of salvation. And these concepts are, perhaps, nearer to our hearts than the conceptual resources of Platonic thought, centering on order and revolving around the cathartic intuition of ideas. . . . *But* without the transmission through socialization and the transformation through philosophy of *any one* of the great world religions, this semantic potential could one day become inaccessible.[47]

Another factor that may have contributed to delaying the reception of Habermas as a philosopher who has contributed to our understanding of religion is certainly the very epochal and pointed character of his contributions. Every major work by Habermas has acted as a catalyst but also as a barometer of the *Zeitgeist*, registering its deepest fears and most cherished hopes.[48] Indeed the polemical and innovative character of Habermas' works over the last forty years militates against trying to link Habermas' position with established and old-fashioned questions like: What about religion? Further, the skewed reception of Habermas' work, especially in the United States, which sometimes echoes to his detriment throughout the world, has also prevented a cross-textual, cross-disciplinary reading of his work. This last factor is particularly surprising given the theoretical claims of Habermas' own research agenda. He has without equivocation continued the interdisciplinary research agenda that informed the Frankfurt School's Critical Theory.

In what follows I will offer a reconstruction of those types of formulations and pronoucements made by Habermas that trace out a historical-developmental, quasi-functionalist, in short phylogenetic, story of the rise and transformation, but not demise, of religion. This type of exegesis and reconstruction is necessary to dispel the misconception of an unambiguous Habermasian rejection of religion. First, I want to show that there have been modifications in Habermas' views on religion. Such variations have to do with the increase in nuance and sophistication of his theoretical model. At the same time, I would like to illustrate the extent to which Habermas has also continued to maintain questions concerning religion close to the center of his thought.[49]

A fuller, more appropriate analysis of Habermas' treatment of religion would have to complement the work here undertaken with what I would call its dialectical complement, namely Habermas' philosophical treatment of religion. Indeed, a parallel reconstruction and exegesis would need to be undertaken which traces those formulations and pronouncements made by Habermas that explicitly articulate how the semantic contents of religion (as well as its institutional dimension, I would say) remain inextinguishable and always still to be non-instrumentally appropriated. While the work I undertake here deals with Habermas the sociologist of religion, the missing dialectical complement would be one that deals with Habermas the philosopher of religion, in whose hands the philosophy of religion turns into the critique of religion. Indeed, such an extended analysis would demonstrate how Habermas the philosopher of religion rescues, preserves, and transforms those views developed by the first generation of the Frankfurt School. While there are substantive differences between the two generations, I suggest that Habermas, for philosophical, cultural, and also political reasons, has continued to make use of the critique of religion I briefly demarcated in the first section of this introduction. For the moment I will briefly mention the way in which Habermas has appealed during the *Historikerstreit* to the Benjaminian idea of anamnesis as not just a philosophical trope but even a civic duty.[50]

The debates about whether Habermas' turn toward the philosophy of language (analytic philosophy), the appropriation of certain motifs from Weber's functionalism and Luhmann's systems theory, and his severe criticisms of Adorno and Horkheimer have transformed him into an apostate, have had the unfortunate consequence of eclipsing the ways in which Habermas' thought has indeed inherited the spirit of the first generation of the Frankfurt School. In fact, the essays I have selected here, guided by Habermas' suggestions as well, ought to constitute evidence for this claim. The texts here selected speak eloquently to that inheritance by retaining its critical approach to religion, even to the extent of criticizing the religion projected by the first generation's critique of religion. In other words, Habermas remains true to the spirit of Horkheimer's and Adorno's critique of religion in his criticism of their own negative theology.

In the widely read and still classic text of 1968, written on the occasion of Herbert Marcuse's seventieth birthday, Habermas already approaches the question of religion. This is a very important text for at least two reasons. First, because Habermas, vis-à-vis the work of Marcuse, seeks to elaborate a critical-theoretical approach to the question of technology in particular, and the growth of the rationalization of society in general. Second, because here is made explicit, if not for the first time, at least in an extended and elaborated fashion, Habermas' own dissatisfaction with the Frankfurt School's traditional approach to the question of the rationalization of society. In this text, in fact, Habermas elaborates more extensively on the distinction between work and interaction, which he had announced in an essay from the same period: "Labor and Interaction: Remarks on Hegel's Jena *Philosophy of Mind*."[51] In this latter essay, Habermas pursues the missed opportunities in Hegel's early work, and how such failures have adverse effects in the development of Marx's own work. In the Marcuse essay, Habermas takes up his philosophical reflections from the angle of social theory. The intent behind the introduction of this distinction is dual. On the one hand, Habermas wanted to disentangle Marcuse's critical theory of technology and societal development from a host of aporias and self-contradictions which nullifed some worthy insights. On the other hand, Habermas wanted to rescue Weber's and Parsons' analysis from their subjectivistic and monological perspectives. Still, the unifying thrust of this distinction is to allow for an appropriate understanding of the logics that inform the rationalization of different modes of action. In this early sketch, "labor" refers to purposive action which brings together instrumental and/or rational choice. Such forms of action are guided by technical rules, or strategies of either maximization of benefits or minimization of costs. By "interaction," Habermas understands what he already called, in the late 1960s, *communicative action*, that is, that type of action that is guided by binding *consensual norms*. Succinctly, as Habermas put it: "While the validity of technical rules and strategies depends on that of empirically true or analytically correct propositions, the validity of social norms is grounded only in the intersubjectivity of the mutual understanding of intentions and secured by the general recognition of obligations."[52] This analytical distinction actually corresponds to different social systems. Social systems, or societal contexts for interaction, differ and are differentiated on whether they are the locus for the predominance of one or the other mode of action. This mapping of modes of action to social systems allowed Habermas to distinguish between (1) the institutional framework of society or what he calls the lifeworld, and (2) the subsystems of purposive-rational, or instrumental, action. With this distinction to hand, Habermas proceeds to reconstruct Weber's theory of the rationalization of society, with an eye, as well, to correcting the misguided appropriation of Weber by the first generation of critical theorists.

Max Weber's social theory is above all a theory of the phylogenesis of social systems and their corresponding forms of rationality. Weber's theory, as Habermas is going to make explicit in his *Theory of Communicative Action*, is a theory of society as a theory of rationality, which in turn must be specified as the theory of the differentiation of types of rationality, or typology of rationality. This much was already clear to the young Habermas in this early incursion into the reconstruction of historical materialism. In this early essay from 1968, therefore, Habermas will offer a sketch of a succession of different developmental stages of human societies to match his analytical distinction between life-world and systems level. Habermas distinguishes among archaic, primitive, traditional, and modern or post-conventional societies. Traditional societies differ from archaic or primitive societies in that traditional societies: (1) have developed centralized ruling powers, (2) have divided vertically into socioeconomic casts or groups, (3) have developed centralized worldviews to legitimate centralized powers and the distribution of social goods. But what is true about the distinction between archaic and traditional societies is also true of the distinction between traditional and modern societies. Their differences can be gauged by the asymmetry between the harnessing of productive forces, and the dictates and goals of legitimation strategies of force and coercion, and how the latter are overtaken by the former. Differences in societal development are partly determined by the gap that develops between the extension and levels of sophistication in the subsystem of purposive-instrumental action and the legitimation of power.[53]

Indeed, the triumph of capitalism within modern societies has to do with its relative success at harmonizing and bringing into equilibrium the divergent trends of the expansion of subsystems of instrumental action and the legitimation of coercion. This is what Weber called the rationalization of the forms of interaction. In Habermas' view, however, it has to be made explicit that this rationalization is executed or brought about from "above" and "below." From below, by the very success of the subsystems of instrumental action that, with each gain, continue to expand vertically, taking over more and more subsystems of purposive or instrumental action. Progressively and ineluctably every major, and minor, structure of traditional society is brought under the logic of instrumental or strategic rationality. Simultaneously, but now as if from "above," world-views, whether mythological or religious, lose their power and "cogency."[54] This rationalization from above is what Weber called secularization. This is made up of two aspects. On the one hand, traditional world-views lose their power and status as myths, rituals, justifying metaphysics, and immutable traditions, as they are interiorized. In this view, secularization means subjectivification, or subjective relativization. On the other hand, secularization also means that such traditions, world-views, rituals, legitimating metaphysics, etc., are transformed "into contructions that do both at once: criticize tradition and reorganize the released material of tradition according to the principles of formal law and the exchange of equivalents (rationalist natural law)."[55] This is a pregnant formulation. Rationalization as secularization means that traditions, or world outlooks, themselves became the locus of contestation and innovation as well as the site for the preservation and transmission of tradition. There are no longer "traditional" world-views that lag behind, as archaic remnants, which are not submitted to the court of rational self-justification. Tradition itself, be it religious or metaphysical, must be rationally justified. Hence the long history of theologizing and metaphysical speculation that accompanies the modernization of world religions. Secularization, in short, means that religious as well as metaphysical outlooks became the site of their own delegitimation and relegitimation. Tradition is discovered as such at the very instant that it becomes open to reconfiguration and rational analysis. For this reason, Habermas notes, "ideologies are coeval with the critique of ideology."[56] Or, formulated in slightly different terms: the tradition of modernity is the critique of tradition for the sake of tradition.[57]

A slightly different version of such an orientation towards the modernity of religion is voiced in Habermas' 1973 work *Legitimation Crisis*.[58] Briefly put, the goal of this work was to translate the discourse about the contradictions of capitalism, as it was articulated by historical materialism, into a discourse about the crises and deficits of the rational legitimation of modernized, secularized, rationalized systems of interaction and the increasingly weakened and demystified world outlooks. In this work, Habermas sought to offer his complement to Marxism, and classical Frankfurt School critical theory, in terms of politics and economics. How do we understand the "contradictions" of a social totality when this totality itself is now conceptually dissected into two distinct levels: the lifeworld and the systems level? Both operate according to their own logics. Their development is dictated by their respective corporealizations of forms of reason, or modes of action. Further, if we understand society diachronically as a differentiated arrangement of types of rationality, then contradictions must now be rethought as crises or pathologies in the forms of rational adjudication and justification. Either insufficient rationalization, or pathological rationalization. It is against this background of the systematic reformulation of the Marxist project of the critique of political economy into a critique of failed or pathological rationalizations of society that Habermas once again broaches the question of religion and, now explicitly, of God.

In the section entitled "The End of the Individual?" Habermas discusses the shipwrecking of world-views on the shoals of the disjunction between the cognitive and social integrative functions of traditional world-views. Indeed, at the minimum, one of the fundamental functions of religious and metaphysical world-views was to integrate individuals into society, by offering bridges between individual and group identity, while offering a cognitive handle on the natural world.[59] With the rationalization of world-views, from above, to use the language of his *Festschrift* essay for Marcuse, personal identity is now separated from group identity, and these in turn are made distinct from any cognitive management of the natural world. In this view, the rationalization of metaphysical and religious world-views means that we must face our subjectivities and group alliances as contingent, for neither entails the other. At the same time, the intractability and resistance of the natural world before our own wills means that we must face our individual existences in the world as entirely contingent. We must face the world *disconsolately*, without warrants or guarantees. In this desolate world, bereft of unifying and mean-ingful mental or religious pictures, are we to surrender to technoc-racy, to disavow the links between truth and justice, and hence, in turn, is a universalistic morality to be reduced to its empty self-affirmation before the scientist and objectifying self-understanding of contemporary humanity?[60]

Habermas speculates that an affirmative answer is not yet forth-coming, if only because of the "repoliticization" of the biblical tradi-tion, as was particularly observable in the then emerging theological formulations of political theologians.[61] Such repoliticization, which entailed a leveling of the immanent/transcendent dichotomy, was not supposed to be read as atheism. Instead, such "religious" revivals, and modern reappropriations of the traditions, formulated from within but also heeding the challenges of the times, are to be understood as modern reformulations of the very concept of God. Habermas writes:

> The idea of God is transformed [*aufgehoben*] into a concept of a *Logos* that determines the community of believers and the real life-context of a self-emancipating society. "God" becomes the name for a com-municative structure that forces men [*sic*], on pain of a loss of their humanity, to go beyond their accidental, empirical nature to encounter one another *indirectly*, that is, across an objective something that they themselves are not.[62]

Evidently, it would be anachronistic, although not illegitimate, to re-read this incredible formulation in the language of *The Theory of Communicative Action*. God is the name for that substance that gives coherence, unity, and thickness to the life-world wherein humans dwell seeking to acknowledge each other as meaning-giving creatures. One may ask, paralleling this reinscription: Is this God the *Logos* of a community of "believers" (who are always believers only insofar as they speak, confess, and bear witness in a community of communi-cation of biblical texts and truths), the same God that is now the communicative rationality of a community of arguers and vulnerable corporealities? And if we answer this question affirmatively, then how must we relate Habermas' reinscription of God to the tradition that sees God as the cipher of humanity's unactualized potentials? In this tradition, God is the name for a negative fiction of what humans should become but are always hindered from becoming by their own corporeality and finitude.

Another key textual point of reference that should be visited before we turn to the pivotal *The Theory of Communicative Action*, is Habermas' synthesizing and synoptic 1976 introduction to his *Zur Rekonstruktion des Historischen Materialismus*, "Historical Materialism and the Development of Normative Structures."[63] This introduction offers a map of Habermas' efforts to reconstruct historical materialism. The text it introduces is itself divided into four major sections: philosophical perspectives, identity, evolution, and legitimation. The introduction, therefore, undertakes the task of unifying what Habermas had been trying to accomplish during the early 1970s, which succinctly and poignantly is summarized by him in the following way: to spell out the ways in which communication theory can contribute to understanding the learning processes that humanity has undergone not just in the dimension of objectivating and instrumentalizing thought, but also in the different dimensions of moral insight, practical knowledge, consensual arbitration of social interaction. In short, Habermas sought to preserve the critical impetus of historical materialism by rearticulating its analysis of human history in terms of a theory of the acquisition of communicative competencies whose developmental logic can be analyzed as a process of rationalization, formalization, universalization and abstraction. The idea, therefore, is to reconstruct the developmental logics of those processes of rationalization that have guided the internal differentiation of processes of identity constitution, social differentiation, and political legitimation. To accomplish this, Habermas draws out what he calls "homologies" between ontogenetic and phylogenetic developmental logics; such homologies are to be traced by comparing the developmental logics of the domains of ego and world-views, on the one hand, and ego and group identities, on the other.[64]

Habermas is quick to qualify the conditions under which these homologies, or parallelisms, can be drawn. He spells out a long and detailed list of the kinds of reservations that must be heeded and specious parallelisms that might be illegitimately drawn. Nonetheless, Habermas goes on, certain homologies can be made explicit. Thus, we are able to discern within the ontogenesis of the cognitive capacities of individuals the following: the differentiation of temporal horizons, namely the differentiation between natural and subjective time; the articulation of the concepts of causality and substance.

Similarly, mythological and religious world-views admit of an analysis that makes explicit the development and acquisition of conceptual and logical differentiations. Myth, which corresponds to an early stage of human evolution, is incorporated within traditional societies in a functional manner. Myths are now supposed to legitimate the authority of the ruling structures. But at that very instant, myth turns into tradition by being assimilated within a temporal horizon. In other words, the very incorporation of myth within the social fabric of a differentiated social system leads to the catalyzing of myth into tradition, which in turn transforms itself into abstract principles upon which argumentative orders are grounded. In the parallel unfolding of logical structures, cognitive competences, ego and group identities, myth and tradition never remain the same, and are never simply ossified. Just as the cognitive competences and faculties of a human being can be understood as the acquisition of more decentered and self-reflexive learning abilities, world-views, religious and metaphysical systems are also caught in the flow of processes of desubstantialization, decentering, and self-reflexivity. At the very moment that universalistic forms of interaction are being established through the triumph of capitalism and the bourgeois political revolutions of the eighteenth century, religious and metaphysical world-views are simultaneously introjected and rendered reflexive.[65] The parallelism, however, is not simply a homology. There is a fundamental link. Ontogenesis must be understood as the unfolding of cognitive capacities which in fact are also learning abilities [*Lernfähigkeiten*]. A cognitive capacity is above all a way of learning. But such learning abilities must be, as Habermas notes, "latently" available in world-views before they may be utilized socially, that is, be "transposed into societal learning processes."[66] Enlightened subjects are not possible without enlightened world-views, like those of the classical monotheistic religions of the Axial Age.[67]

Our chronological analysis of some key sections in Habermas' texts from the late 1960s through the 1970s should have left the clear impression that his project of a reconstruction of historical materialism entailed the salvaging of all kinds of insights from different fields. Viewed in this fashion, Habermas has remained true to the inter-disciplinary project of the Frankfurt School. Practically, this has meant that Habermas has taken recourse to what seem to be *prima facie* antithetical approaches: Hegel, Marx, Gadamer, Adorno, Marcuse, Blumenberg, Koselleck, but also Piaget, Kohlberg,Luhmann,

Weber, Durkheim, and Mead. Here we must recall that many of Habermas' books began as *Literaturberichte* (reports on the literature of a particular debate or field).[68] This approach should not be understood at all as a type of eclecticism, or theoretical promiscuity. Instead, as we have noted thus far, Habermas wants to preserve Marx's insights into history and the pathogenesis of capitalism by translating them into the language of developmental logics and rationalization processes. The point was not to dissolve Marx into Weber, and historical materialism into systems theory, but rather to see whether both could be measured by the same standard: namely the question of humanity's differentiated unfolding, in which the development of cognitive competences are matched by the development in social structures which both preserve and mobilize the learning abilities of human subjects. To this extent, Habermas' theoretical appropriations should be seen as *litmus tests* of the theories themselves. In Habermas' case theoretical reconstructions have a systematic intent in such a way that "for any social theory, linking up with the history of theory is also a kind of test; the more freely it can take up, explain, criticize, and carry on the intentions of earlier theory traditions, the more impervious it is to the danger that particular interests are being brought to bear unnoticed in its own theoretical perspective."[69]

On the question of Habermas' relationship to religion, we note that his analysis remains basically the same, albeit now formulated in terms of a detailed theory of communicative competences and the symbolic acquisition of identity. Whereas in his earlier writings Habermas approached the question of the secularization (i.e. rationalization) of religious and metaphysical world-views through the lens of Weber, Hegel, and his colleagues at Starnberg Klaus Eder and Rainer Döbert, in *The Theory of Communicative Action* Habermas approaches this question through the lenses of Mead's and Durkheim's complementary theoretical models. Just as Habermas had found Hegel, Marx, and Marcuse wanting because of their failure to address the differentiated modes of action, namely instrumental and communicative, now Habermas finds Weber, Adorno, Parsons, and Luhmann also lacking because of their failure to address the question of the unfolding of modes of interaction, their corresponding domains of embodiment, and the acquisition of cognitive capacities in terms of a symbolic, communicative, linguistic understanding of reason and agency. The failures of these great thinkers, suggests Habermas, were to be remedied from within, namely, by making explicit what they already presupposed tacitly. Here, again, Habermas has also remained faithful to the critical orientation of the Frankfurt School, that is, to think from within the very theoretical assumptions of a given analysis or conceptual orientation its own inadequacies.

More concretely, the fundamental question for Habermas in the late 1970s became how we can explain the development of universal and normative structures as the development of linguistic and symbolic competences. This is where Mead and Durkheim are introduced to play a pivotal role. The former allows Habermas to reconstruct his theory of individuation as a theory of language acquisition, which holds that subjectivity comes after an intersubjectivity that is co-originary with the acquisition of language. Mead turns into the Hegel and Kierkegaard of Habermas' new theory of subjectivity, or more accurately of communicative agency. Durkheim, on the other hand, allows Habermas to reconstruct the development of normative social order as the process of symbolic integration that is matched by social solidarity. Durkheim allows Habermas to translate Weber's and Parsons' question about order into a question about the symbolic constitution of social solidarity, and the symbolic integration of individuals into social groups. In tandem, Habermas must discuss the way in which world-views, whether metaphysical or religious, are linguistified, that is, rendered accessible to symbolically constituted agents through being opened up to discursive or linguistic treatment. Thus, in this expanded theoretical orientation, the separation between the profane and sacred corresponds to a split in the medium of communication, namely the split that takes place between the propositional, expressive, and normative uses of language that correspond to objective nature, the social, and subjective worlds respectively.[70]

In order to accomplish his theoretical aims, Habermas must explain how religious and metaphysical world-views, which at early or so-called archaic stages provided an analogical coordination between nature, humanity, and society, became a "drive belt that transforms the basic religious consensus into the energy of social solidarity and passes it onto social institutions, thus giving them a moral authority."[71] Religious world-views, in fact, hasten the process of the sublimation of the compulsive power of terrifying divine power into the normative binding power of social norms. It is not that political or social power compels religion to surrender its grip over the cowed masses; rather, inasmuch as religion itself is ritualized, and then made part of a tradition, which is then reflexively appropriated and rendered accessible to criticism, religion itself compels subjects to adopt universalizing and critical attitudes towards its own myths and theologemes. Habermas makes this explicit when he writes, and I must quote at length:

> The core of collective consciousness is a normative consensus established and regenerated in the ritual practices of a community of believers. Members thereby orient themselves to religious symbols; the intersubjective unity of the collective presents itself to them in concepts of the holy. This collective identity defines the circle of those who understand themselves as members of the same social group and can speak of themselves in the first-person plural. The symbolic actions of the rites can be comprehended as residues of a stage of communication that has already been gone beyond in domains of profane social cooperation.[72]

Through a religious symbol, or a theologumenon, a community of believers, which is also a ritual community, constitutes itself as a group. This clears up the linguistic space for the first-person plural pronouncements. Simultaneously, this linguistic circumscription initiates the separation of the sacred from the profane. Everyday practice is desacralized. Religion, as belief and ritual (that is, practice) inaugurated a particular syntactical relation that in turn overtook it.[73] *Religion linguistifies the world, catalyzing the very dichotomies that in turn linguistify the sacred.* The power exercised by myth over humans is transformed into the non-coercive coercion of moral norms. The religious is not so much disposed and left behind, but rather internalized in society; it allows for society to take place. The normative power harbored and protected within religious contexts is released through communicative action. "Only in and through communicative action can the energies of social solidarity attached to religious symbolism branch out and be imparted, in the form of moral authority, both to institutions and to persons."[74]

Only the disenchantment and disempowerment of the sacred domain through its linguistification leads to the release of the binding, normative power stored in its ritualistically accomplished normative agreements.[75] This also releases the rational potential implied in communicative action. For, the "aura of rapture and terror that emanates from the sacred, the *spellbinding* power of the holy, is sublimated into the *binding/bonding* force of criticizable validity claims and at the same time turned into an everyday occurrence."[76] The linguistification of the sacred leads to its dialectical assimilation and transformation. The compulsion exercised by the "wholly Other" turns into an everyday occurrence which we must live by in terms of our respect for the binding force of norms of action and moral maxims. Indeed, only a universalistic, deontic, moral outlook that corresponds to a post-conventional moral outlook can appropriate the normative contents of religion: "neither science nor art can inherit the mantle of religion; only a morality, set communicatively aflow and developed into a discourse ethics, can replace the authority of the sacred."[77]

After almost half a century of public intellectual and scientific work, Habermas' contribution is both impressive and humbling. Habermas has remained vital, creative, engaged, and most importantly attuned to the *Zeitgeist*, without sacrificing intellectual honesty and rigor. There is no field that he has left untouched, and this includes religion, even if in this his reception has been mixed and skewed. As questions of pluralism, cross-cultural dialogue, fundamentalisms, reassessments of notions of inalienable rights and sacredness of life, religiously fueled conflicts, continue to press upon contemporary life, Habermas' insights into religion can offer a guide, and point of debate. In an age of so-called globalization, the "West" itself has been provincialized, rendered local and historically contingent. Globalization has meant that the "West" has now to give an account of itself, to others, as well as to itself. Giving such an account must begin, above all, with a discussion of the West's relationship to its religious identity.[78] It is against this background that Habermas' wide-ranging, systematic, sociologically and philosophically informed analyses of religion commend themselves. In the brief and focused reconstruction executed above, traces and points of entry for a thoughtful engagement were offered. At the very least, this reconstruction should make it more difficult to accept quick dismissals of Habermas' insights into religion. Habermas is certainly a secularist, but he is no anti-religion *philosophe*. "As long as no better words for what religion can say are found in the medium of rational discourse, it [communicative reason] will even coexist abstemiously with the former, neither supporting it nor combatting it."[79]

Athens or Jerusalem

The essays here gathered were selected from a variety of sources which are either no longer available, have never been available in translation, or are not widely known. The essays span four decades, and cover a variety of themes and philosophemes that, as can be seen from the selection, have remained central in Habermas' intellectual itinerary. The book opens with a classic essay, originally written as a radio program, on the relationship between German philosophy and Jewish philosophers. What is striking, other than the breadth of Habermas' knowledge about the interaction between Jewish and German thought, is the sense of moral urgency and indignation with which Habermas approached the question. What was to become so significant during the Historians' Dispute is here already made patently clear, namely the imperative to take the Holocaust as a historical index of radical evil that can never lose its singularity regardless of historicist explanations. The next essay, a review of Klaus Heinrich's book *Versuch über die Schwierigkeit, Nein zu sagen* [*Essay on the Difficulty of Saying No*], included here at Habermas' urging, presages two central motifs in Habermas' future development. First, the relationship between rationalization and mythological or religious world-views, in which the latter must submit to the transformative criticism enacted by the former. And, second, that if we are to understand human development at all we must be attentive to the ways in which gains in inter-human relationships are co-ordinated and preserved through the medium of language. The logic of instrumentalization by means of which we control nature is different from the thrust towards emancipation that is unleashed by the process of rationalization of linguistically mediated communication and interaction.

The next essay, "Transcendence from Within, Transcendence in this World," is the text of Habermas' response to a conference organized by Phil Devenish and Don S. Browning at the Divinity School of the University of Chicago, October 7–9, 1988. The title of the conference was: "Critical Theory: Its Promises and Limitations for a Theology of the Public Realm." Among the numerous participants were many important theologians and philosophers of religion, such as Fred Dallmayr, Francis Schüssler Fiorenza, Matthew Lamb, Helmut Peukert, Gary M. Simpson, David Tracy, Robert Wuthnow, Sheila

Briggs, and others.[80] Here Habermas responded to sometimes very pointed and substantial criticisms, although the theologians would have welcome a more direct engagement of their objections and concerns. The key idea in this text, however, is Habermas' affirmation of "methodical atheism" as the only acceptable option for postmetaphysical and enlightened philosophy. This option seeks not only to salvage philosophy as it navigates between the "Scylla of a leveling, transcendence-less empiricism and the Charybdis of a high-flying idealism that glories transcendence" (see page 91 in this volume). It also seeks to salvage the religious from philosophy's, or any other discipline's, illegitimate and surreptitious appropriation. Here Habermas reaffirms his stand enunciated in his book *Postmetaphysical Thinking*, and to paraphrase, as long as religion can still say something that philosophy cannot, then philosophy, even in its postmetaphysical form, will not be able either to replace or to repress religion. The essay bearing as its title Horkheimer's statement "To seek to salvage an unconditional meaning without God is a futile undertaking" was written on the occasion of Alfred Schmidt's sixtieth birthday. With his usual thoroughness, Habermas reconstructs the intellectual genealogy that gave rise to such an expression. Habermas demonstrates, however, how Horkheimer has made a category mistake, if his statement is meant in the negative sense that indeed it is futile to seek an unconditional meaning without God, that is, that indeed nothing else is worth pursuing without such a divine warrant. What Horkheimer demands in this negative sense is to obtain from philosophy something that is not forthcoming from it. Philosophy has never and can never be a source of existential consolation. Furthermore, as Habermas points out, whoever has made a linguistic pronouncement has already submitted himself to the tribunal of justificatory discourse. No communicative act is exempt from criticism, and as such they are all always revisable and rejectable. It is in this latter sense, then, that we can read positively Horkheimer's statement.

The essay entitled "Communicative Freedom and Negative Theology. Questions to Michael Theunissen" takes up again the challenge of a possible postmetaphysical appropriation of the Christian philosophical tradition, but now from the standpoint of a negative dialectics elaborated as Hellenization of Christianity. This essay, therefore should be read as a counterpoint to the other essays where Habermas deals with the same project, but as it would be elaborated from the standpoint of a Judification of Christianity, as has been pursued by Johannes Baptist Metz. Habermas is sympathetic to, although ultimately critical of, Theunissen's attempts to render a postmetaphysical version of a philosophical justification and translation of the Christian promise of salvation. Theunissen, in Habermas' reconstruction, articulates a formidable and suggestive elaboration of the links between Marx and Kierkegaard, and the extension of a left-leaning, existentialist critique of Hegel. Theunissen also develops out of the same sources something which has remained unelaborated in Habermas' own work, namely the idea of "communicative freedom,"[81] but which he finds suggestive and indicative of a line of philosophical investigation that must be pursued.

In the next essay, on Gershom Scholem, Habermas revisits the work of a colleague who, Habermas has admitted, was one of his spiritual teachers.[82] In this essay, Habermas traces a duality in Scholem's work, which is not unlike the one traced above with respect to Horkheimer's and Adorno's relationship to religion. This duality is tinged with rational resignation and spiritual nostalgia. On the one hand, Scholem as a historian of Jewish messianism and religious thought has masterfully dominated all the techniques of historical investigation we have inherited from the scientific Enlightenment. He is no less a child of the Enlightenment because the object of his investigations is the rescue of a tradition that has apparently been lost. On the other hand, Scholem is no dispassionate and disinterested investigator. However, as Habermas points out, Scholem is aware that we cannot retreat behind the Enlightenment, and that the change that religion, in particular mysticism, has undergone through its transformation into political utopianism and religious nihilism, has been both unavoidable and unsatisfactory.[83] The last essay was written on the occasion of Johannes Baptist Metz's retirement from teaching, and it may be considered both a response and a challenge. In this essay Habermas defends the legitimacy of the historical marriage between Christianity and Hellenism, where both stand metonymically for two seemingly irreconcilable forces: logos and memory. But the historically obtained synthesis between these two forces, captured aptly in Metz's term "anamnestic reason," if it is not to betray either of its sources, must not be left to theologians alone. Philosophy itself must translate the contents of that *philotheologumenon*: anamnestic reason. Furthermore, and this is Habermas' challenge, without the secularization and transformation which are enacted by philosophy's translation from religious to secular concepts, the religious itself would remain mute and even threaten to petrify and remain historically ineffective. Without philosophy, what lives in religion might perish, or remain inaccessible to us children of the Enlightenment.[84]

The book closes with an interview I conducted with Habermas specifically for this book. Each question was inspired by motifs that are dispersed throughout the different essays in this book, but also by issues that have become more pressing in the recent past: the question of globalization and its relationship to religious fundamentalism, Habermas' relationship to the Jewish aspects of the first Frankfurt School's Critical Theory, his appraisal of the challenge of liberation theology, and the philosophical relevance of religious language in contemporary society. This interview might be taken as Habermas' most up-to-date statement on the question of religion in modern society and its relationship to the Judeo-Christian tradition that has so thoroughly impacted one of the richest traditions of critical thought. It would not be inappropriate to conclude this introduction by paraphrasing Kant, by way of both Adorno and Bloch. In Habermas' view, religion without philosophy is speechless, philosophy without religion is contentless; both remain irreducible as long as we must face our anthropological vulnerability without consolation, without ultimate guarantees.

Eduardo Mendieta

Acknowledgments

I want to thank Santiago Castro-Gómez, Martin Matustik, Matthias Lütkehermölle, and Reyes Mate for their comments on earlier versions of this introduction. I also want to thank the anonymous readers for Polity, whose suggestions substantively improved this text.

Notes

1   See Jürgen Habermas, "A Genealogical Analysis of the Cognitive Content of Morality," in his *The Inclusion of the Other: Studies in Political Theory* (Cambridge: Polity, 1999), 3–46.
2   Albert Schweitzer, *The Quest of the Historical Jesus. A Critical Study of its Progress from Reimarus to Wrede*, trans. W. Montgomery (London: A. & C. Black, Ltd. 1936), 1.

3 Theodor W. Adorno, *Negative Dialectics*, trans. E. B. Ashton (New York: Continuum, 1983), 365.

4 Michael Löwy, *Redemption and Utopia: Jewish Libertarian Thought in Central Europe. A Study in Elective Affinity*, trans. Hope Heaney (Stanford: Stanford University Press, 1992).

5 Gershom Scholem, *On Jews and Judaism in Crisis. Selected Essays*, ed. Werner J. Dannhauser (New York: Shocken Books, 1976), 287.

6 In addition to the works already mentioned, we need to add Michael Löwy, *On Changing The World. Essays in Political Philosophy, from Karl Marx to Walter Benjamin* (Atlantic Highlands, NJ and London: Humanities Press, 1992), and Reyes Mate, *Memoria de Occidente. Actualidad de pensadores judíos olvidados* (Barcelona: Editorial Anthropos, 1997).

7 See Anson Rabinbach, "Between Enlightenment and Apocalypse: Benjamin, Bloch and Modern German Jewish Messianism," *New German Critique*, 34 (Winter 1985), 78–124. See also the extended discussion of the relationship between Jews and Germans in Richard Wolin's important forthcoming book *Heidegger's Children* (Princeton: Princeton University Press, 2001), especially the first chapter, "The German–Jewish Dialogue: Way Stations of Misrecognition."

8 See Löwy, *Redemption and Utopia*, 34.

9 See the excellent essay by Zygmunt Bauman, "Exit Visas and Entry Tickets: Paradoxes of Jewish Assimilation," *Telos*, 77 (Fall 1988), 45–77.

10 Rabinbach, "Between Enlightenment and Apocalypse," 87.

11 See Rudolf J. Siebert, *The Critical Theory of Religion: From Universal Pragmatic to Political Theology* (Berlin, New York, Amsterdam: Mouton Publishers, 1985). See also the short studies gathered in Wilhelm Schmidt, ed., *Die Religion der Religionskritik* (Munich: Claudius Verlag, 1972); Edmund Arens, Ottmar John, and Peter Rottländer, *Erinnerung, Befreiung, Solidarität: Benjamin, Marcuse, Habermas und die politische Theologie* (Düsseldorf: Patmos Verlag, 1991); see also Edmund Arens, "Interruptions: Critical Theory and Political Theology between Modernity and Postmodernity," in David Batstone et al., *Liberation Theologies, Postmodernity, and the Americas* (New York: Routledge, 1997), 222–42.

12 See Rudolf J. Siebert, *Horkheimer's Critical Sociology of Religion: The Relative and the Transcendent* (Washington, D.C.: University Press of America, 1979). See also the excellent introduction to the Spanish translation of some of Horkheimer's writings on religion by Juan José Sánchez, in Max Horkheimer, *Anhelo de Justicia: Teoría crítica y religión*, ed. Juan José Sánchez (Madrid: Editorial Trotta, 2000).

13 The works of Rudolf Siebert, Michael Löwy, Reyes Mate, and José Mardones are substantive contributions in the direction of an exclusive study of the critique of religion by the Frankfurt School. While Siebert's is oriented toward philosophy, and in particular Hegel's philosophy of

religion, Löwy's is oriented toward the elective affinity of Judaism and libertarian utopianism in the early part of the twentieth century.

14 See the interview with Helmut Gumnior, "Die Sehnsucht nach dem ganz Anderen," in *Gesammelte Schriften*, vol. 7 *Vorträge und Aufzeichnungen 1949–1973*, ed. Gunzelin Schmid Noerr (Frankfurt am Main: S. Fischer Verlag, 1985), 398.

15 Adorno, *Negative Dialectics*, 397.

16 Martin Jay, *The Dialectical Imagination: A History of the Frankfurt School and the Institute for Social Research 1923–1950* (Boston and Toronto: Little, Brown and Company, 1973), xii.

17 See Löwy, *Redemption and Utopia*, 127. Lukács used the expression with reference to Dostoyevsky.

18 Scholem, *On Jews and Judaism in Crisis*, 46.

19 On Walter Benjamin's thinking from the standpoint of theology and Judaism see the following sources: Susan Buck-Morss, *The Origin of Negative Dialectics: Theodor W. Adorno, Walter Benjamin, and the Frankfurt Institute* (New York: The Free Press, 1977), and her *The Dialectics of Seeing: Walter Benjamin and the Arcades Project* (Cambridge, MA: MIT Press, 1989); Peter Szondi, "Hope in the Past: On Walter Benjamin," *Critical Inquiry*, 4, 3 (Spring 1978), 491–506; Rolf Tiedemann, "Historical Materialism or Political Messianism? An Interpretation of the Theses "On the Concept of History," *Philosophical Forum*, XV, 1–2 (Fall–Winter 1983–4), 71–104; Christian Lenhardt, "Anamnestic Solidarity: The Proletariat and its *Manes*," *Telos*, 25 (Fall 1975), 133–54. On Ernst Bloch, see Gerard Raulet, "Critique of Religion and Religion as Critique: The Secularized Hope of Ernst Bloch," *New German Critique*, 9 (Fall 1976), 71–85; Richard H. Roberts, *Hope and Its Hieroglyphs: A Critical Interpretation of Ernst Bloch's Principle of Hope* (Atlanta, GA: Scholars Press, 1989), and of course Jürgen Habermas' essays on both Walter Benjamin and Ernst Bloch in his *Philosophical-Political Profiles*, trans. Frederick G. Lawrence (Cambridge, MA: MIT Press, 1983).

20 Although one may argue that toward the end of his life, after his return to Germany, Max Horkheimer increased his preoccupation and statements about religion. As my friend Martin Matustik suggested to me, there might be a correlation between Horkheimer's political conservatism and his religious mysticism. It is true that Horkheimer became almost virulently conservative. Some of his statements make him sound like a religious fundamentalist; for instance, he opposed the pill, abortion, and I suspect also the hedonism and libertinage of the New Left.

21 See the numerous aphorisms on religion, Christianity, Judaism, theology, and so on in Max Horkheimer, *Dawn & Decline: Notes 1926–1931 & 1950–1969*, trans. Michael Shaw (New York: Seabury Press, 1978).

22 Max Horkheimer, "Theism and Atheism," [1963] in *Critique of Instrumental Reason*, trans. Matthew J. O'Connell et al. (New York: Continuum, 1974), 47–8. Now in *Gesammelte Schriften*, vol. 7, 173–86.

23 Horkheimer, *Gesammelte Schriften*, vol. 7, 276.

24 This has already been done in Spanish. See the wonderful collection of Max Horkheimer's writing on religion: Max Horheimer, *Anhelo de Justicia: teoría crítica y religión*, ed. Juan José Sánchez (Madrid: Editorial Trotta, 2000).

25 See Horkheimer, *Critique of Instrumental Reason*, 113; and *Gesammelte Schriften*, vol. 7, 387.

26 Horkheimer, *Dawn & Decline*, 239. Tellingly, this sentence, written towards the end of his life, is to be found in the section entitled "The Difference between Critical Theory and the Idea of Faith."

27 See Arnold Künzli, "Irrationalism of the Left," in Judith Marcus and Zoltán Tar, eds., *Foundations of the Frankfurt School of Social Research* (New Brunswick, NJ: Transaction Books, 1984), 133–54.

28 Walter Benjamin, *The Arcades Project*, trans. Howard Eiland and Kevin McLaughlin (Cambridge: The Belknap Press of Harvard University Press, 1999), 471. In the citation format of the Passagen-Werk, N7a,7.

29 Theodor W. Adorno and Walter Benjamin, *The Complete Correspondence 1928–1940*, ed. Henri Lonitz, trans. Nicholas Walker (Cambridge: Polity, 1999), 108.

30 Theodor W. Adorno, *Critical Models: Interventions and Catchwords*, trans. Henry W. Pickford (New York: Columbia University Press, 1998), 139.

31 See Adorno's discussion of the relationship between metaphysics and theology in his lectures from 1965: Theodor W. Adorno, *Metaphysics. Begriff und Probleme (1965) Nachgelassene Schriften. Band 14* (Frankfurt am Main: Suhrkamp Verlag, 1998), 9–22.

32 On Adorno and religion, see Rudolf J. Siebert, "Adorno's Theory of Religion," *Telos*, 58 (Winter 1983–4), 108–14, and Wayne Whitson Floyd, Jr., *Theology and the Dialectics of Otherness: On Reading Bonhöffer and Adorno* (Lanham, MD: University Press of America, 1988).

33 Adorno, *Negative Dialectics*, 400.

34 Ibid, 401–2.

35 Adorno, *Critical Models*, 142.

36 Theodor W. Adorno, *Minima Moralia*, trans. E. F. N. Jephcott (London: New Left Books, 1974), 98.

37 See "Something's Missing: A Discussion between Ernst Bloch and Theodor W. Adorno on the Contradictions of Utopian Longing," in Ernst Bloch, *The Utopian Function of Art and Literature. Selected Essays*, trans. Jack Zipes and Frank Mecklenburg (Cambridge, MA: MIT Press, 1988), 12.

38   Ibid, 16.
39   Ibid.
40   See Reyes Mate, "Thinking in Spanish: Memory of Logos?" *Nepantla: Views from the South*, 2, 2 (Fall 2001), 247–64; see also chapter 3, "Dreaming up Solidarity: Feminist Witnessing and the Community of the *Ought to Be*," in Drucilla Cornell's book *Legacies of Dignity* (New York: Palgrave, 2002).
41   See Edmund Arens, ed., *Habermas und die Theologie: Beiträge zur theologischen Rezeption, Diskussion und Kritik der Theorie kommunikativen Handelns* (Düsseldorf: Patmos Verlag, 1989); Edmund Arens, Ottmar John, and Peter Rottländer, *Erinnerung, Befreiung, Solidarität: Benjamin, Marcuse, Habermas und die politische Theologie* (Düsseldorf: Patmos, 1991); Edmund Arens, ed., *Kommunikatives Handeln und christlicher Glaube. Ein theologischer Diskurs mit Jürgen Habermas* (Paderborn: Ferdinand Schöningh, 1997); Helmut Peukert, *Science, Action, and Fundamental Theology*, trans. James Bohman (Cambridge, Mass: MIT Press, 1984); Don S. Browning and Francis Schüssler Fiorenza, eds., *Habermas, Modernity, and Public Theology* (New York: Crossroad, 1992). See the following works for extended applications of Habermas's theories to theology: Paul Lakeland, *Theology and Critical Theory: The Discourse of the Church* (Nashville: Abingdon Press, 1990), and Jens Glebe-Moller, *A Political Dogmatic* (Philadelphia: Fortress Press, 1987).
42   See the works by Rudolf Siebert, which unfortunately remain barely accessible because of their demanding Hegelian language.
43   See, for instance, the essays collected in Browning and Fiorenza, *Habermas, Modernity, and Public Theology*, already cited above (n. 41). See also Donald Jay Rothberg, "Rationality and Religion in Habermas' Recent Work: Some Remarks on the Relation between Critical Theory and the Phenomenology of Religion," *Philosophy and Social Criticism*, 11 (1986), 221–46; Klaus M. Kodalle, "Zur religionsphilosophischen Auseinandersetzung mit Jürgen Habermas' 'Theorie des kommunikativen Handelns'," *Allgemeine Zeitschrift für Philosophie*, 12 (1987), 39–66; Ludwig Nagl, "Aufhebung der Theologie in der Diskurstheorie? Kritische Anmerkungen zur Religionskritik von Jürgen Habermas," in Herta Nagl-Docekal, ed., *Überlieferung und Aufgabe. Festschrift für Erich Heintel* (Vienna: Wilhelm Braumüller Verlag, 1982), 197–213; Anne Fortin-Melkevik, "The Reciprocal Exclusiveness of Modernity and Religion among Contemporary Thinkers: Jürgen Habermas and Marcel Gauchet," in Claude Geffré and Jean-Pierre Jossua, eds., *The Debate on Modernity. Concilium 1992.6.* (London: SCM Press, 1992), 57–66.
44   I am refering to Habermas's statements of criticism against Jacques Derrida. See Jürgen Habermas, *The Philosophical Discourse of Modernity: Twelve Lectures*, trans. Frederick Lawrence (Cambridge: Polity, 1987), 183–4; see also n. 46, pp. 406–7.

45   While it is neither necessary nor desirable that everyone who writes on contemporary philosophy should write something that in one way or another faces up to the challenges of Habermas, it is indeed unfortunate that in otherwise superlative works like those of John D. Caputo and Hent de Vries no attempt was made to directly address Habermas' criticisms of Derrida's "athestic messianism and mysticism." See John D. Caputo, *The Prayers and Tears of Jacques Derrida: Religion without Religion* (Bloomington and Indianapolis: Indiana University Press, 1997), and Hent de Vries, *Philosophy and the Turn to Religion* (Baltimore and London: The Johns Hopkins University Press, 1999).

46   Habermas, *The Philosophical Discourse of Modernity*, 406–7, n. 46, last sentence.

47   Jürgen Habermas, *Postmetaphysical Thinking: Philosophical Essays*, trans. William Mark Hohengarten (Cambridge: Polity, 1992), 15 (bold added, italics in original). Compare what Habermas says in "The Unity of Reason in the Diversity of Voices" later in the same book, especially p. 145.

48   See Robert C. Holub, *Jürgen Habermas: Critic in the Public Sphere* (London and New York: Routledge, 1991); Max Pensky, "Universalism and the Situated Critic," in Stephen K. White, ed., *The Cambridge Companion to Habermas* (Cambridge: Cambridge University Press, 1995), 67–94; Lewis Edwin Hann, ed., *Perspectives on Habermas* (Chicago and La Salle, IL: Open Court, 2000); see also Martin J. Beck Matustik, *Jürgen Habermas: A Philosophical-Political Profile* (Lanham, Maryland: Rowman & Littlefield Publishers, Inc., 2001).

49   I have been aided in the following reconstruction by the outstanding study of José M. Mardones, *El Discurso religioso de la modernidad. Habermas y la religión* (Barcelona: Editorial Anthropos, 1998).

50   See Jürgen Habermas, "Concerning the Public Use of History," *New German Critique*, 44 (Spring/Summer 1988), 44. In German, see Jürgen Habermas, *Eine Art Schadensabwicklung* (Frankfurt am Main: Suhrkamp Verlag, 1987). See also "On the Public Use of History," in Jürgen Habermas, *The Postnational Constellation: Political Essays* (Cambridge: Polity, 2001), 26–37.

51   Jürgen Habermas, *Theory and Practice*, trans. John Viertel (Boston: Beacon Press, 1973), 142–69.

52   Jürgen Habermas, *Toward a Rational Society: Student Protest, Science, and Politics* (Boston: Beacon Press, 1970), 92.

53   Ibid, 97.

54   Ibid, 98.

55   Ibid, 99.

56   Ibid.

57   See the excellent work by Juan Luis Segundo, *The Liberation of Dogma: Faith, Revelation, and Dogmatic Teaching Authority*, trans. Phillip

Berryman (Maryknoll, NY: Orbis Books, 1992). The original title, *El Dogma Que Libera*, was lost in translation. But the entire book is precisely about a tradition that instigates criticism in its very process of transmission.

58 Jürgen Habermas, *Legitimation Crisis*, trans. Thomas McCarthy (Boston: Beacon Press, 1975).

59 Ibid, 118.

60 Ibid, 120.

61 Habermas mentions Pannenberg, Metz, Moltmann, and Sölle, but one should also add Bloch and Benjamin, who directly and deeply influenced this first generation of political theologians. See *Legitimation Crisis*, 121. See also Habermas' discussions with some theologians transcribed in Dorothee Sölle et al., *Religionsgespräche. Zur gesellschaftlichen Rolle der Religion* (Darmstadt and Neuwied: Hermann Luchterhand Verlag, 1975). See also the references to political theology in *Theorie und Praxis: Sozialphilosophische Studien* (Frankfurt am Main: Suhrkamp Verlag, 1993), 418ff.

62 Habermas, *Legitimation Crisis*, 121. Italics in original. Compare the following statement from Habermas' 1974 speech on the occasion of his receiving the Hegel Prize, which is granted by the city of Stuttgart: "God indicates only approximately a structure of communication, which forces participants, on the foundation of the reciprocal acknowledgment of their identity, to transcend the contingency of a merely external existence" (*Zur Rekonstruktion des Historischen Materialismus* (Frankfurt am Main: Suhrkamp Verlag, 1976), 101). This speech was partly translated as "On Social Identity," *Telos*, 19 (Spring 1974), 91–103.

63 Published in English in Jürgen Habermas, *Communication and the Evolution of Society*, trans. Thomas McCarthy (Boston: Beacon Press, 1979), 95–129.

64 Ibid, 99.

65 Habermas, *Communication and the Evolution of Society*, 105.

66 Ibid, 121.

67 This is Karl Jaspers' term, see his *The Origin and Goal of History* (New Haven, CN: Yale University Press, 1957). For Jaspers the Axial Age represented a radical transformation in the relationship between humans and the cosmos, and humans and their own self-consciousness. During the Axial Age, humans became conscious of Being *qua* Being, but also of human consciousness. At the same time, humanity recognized its ability to comprehend everything, while simultaneously recognizing its own limitations. The most important aspect of this dual recognition is that universality became a normative ideal, that is, a standard but also a goal.

68 See in particular Jürgen Habermas, *Zur Logik der Sozialwissenschaften.*
    Erweiterte Ausgabe (Frankfurt am Main: Suhrkamp Verlag, 1985). This
    book originally appeared in 1970, but was later expanded in 1982.
    The English translation omits much of this text and focuses only on
    the second section of the German version, namely the section on
    hermeneutics.
69 Jürgen Habermas, *The Theory of Communicative Action. Volume One.
    Reason and the Rationalization of Society*, trans. Thomas McCarthy
    (Cambridge: Polity, 1984), 140.
70 See Jürgen Habermas, *The Theory of Communicative Action. Volume Two.
    Lifeworld and System: A Critique of Functionalist Reason*, trans. Thomas
    McCarthy (Cambridge: Polity, 1987), 54. Note that this conceptual-
    ization of the differentiation of religious outlooks in terms of a
    differentiation of linguistic and verbal modes was already elaborated
    by Döbert in the early 1970s. What differs, now, in Habermas's treat-
    ment is that this "linguistic" understanding is backed by a full-fledged
    "universal pragmatics," that is, a theory that describes language
    and reason in terms of validity claims, domains of action, and forms of
    rationality.
71 Ibid, 56.
72 Ibid, 60.
73 Readers of Habermas might be unfamiliar with the voluminous litera-
    ture that makes these claims plausible and credible. For a point of entry
    into the idea that the religious linguistifies and is linguistified, see John
    Dominic Crossan's numerous books, in particular *In Parables: The Chal-
    lenge of the Historical Jesus* (New York: Harper & Row, 1973); *The Dark
    Interval: Towards a Theology of Story* (Niles, IL: Argus, 1975); *The Cross
    That Spoke: The Origins of the Passion Narrative* (San Francisco: Harper
    & Row, 1988). For a comprehensive and systematic overview of the
    impact of the "linguistic turn" on Bible studies, and religion in general,
    see The Bible and Culture Collective, *The Postmodern Bible* (New
    Haven, CN: Yale University Press, 1995).
74 Habermas, *The Theory of Communicative Action*, vol. 2, p. 61.
75 Ibid, 77. This is a paraphrase of the original German, see Jürgen
    Habermas, *Theorie des kommunikativen Handelns. Band 2. Zur Kritik
    der funktionalistischen Vernunft* (Frankfurt am Main: Suhrkamp Verlag,
    1981), 119.
76 Habermas, *The Theory of Communicative Action, Volume Two*, 77. Trans-
    lation slightly altered. The original reads: "Die Aura des Entzückens
    und Erschreckens, die vom Sakralen ausstrahlt, die *bannende* Kraft des
    Heiligen wird zum *bindenden* Kraft kritisierbaren Geltungsansprüchen
    zugleich sublimiert und veralltäglicht" (*Theorie des kommunikativen
    Handelns*, 119).

77 Ibid, 92. Compare Marcel Gauchet, *The Disenchantment of the World: A Political History of Religion*, trans. Oscar Burge (Princeton: Princeton University Press, 1997). For Gauchet, the departure of the gods from the world means the turn inward. The otherness of the gods is replaced by the otherness that the aesthetic experience grants us. Religion is replaced by art, the prophet by the artist, the priest by the cultural critic.

78 See Jacques Derrida, "Faith and Knowledge: The Two Sources of 'Religion' at the Limits of Reason Alone," in Jacques Derrida and Gianni Vattimo, eds., *Religion* (Stanford: Stanford University Press, 1998), 1–78.

79 Habermas, *Postmetaphysical Thinking*, 145.

80 Most of the papers can be found in Don S. Browning and Francis Schüssler Fiorenza, eds., *Habermas, Modernity, and Public Theology* (New York: Crossroads, 1992); for a slightly overlapping German version of this book, see Edmund Arens, eds., *Habermas und Theologie* (Düsseldorf: Patmos, 1989). This was not the first or the last time that Habermas has met and debated with theologians. See Sölle et al., *Religionsgespräche*, and more recently, Edmund Arens, ed., *Kommunikatives Handeln und christlicher Glaube. Ein theologischer Diskurs mit Jürgen Habermas* (Paderborn: Ferdinand Schöningh, 1997).

81 Here I can only direct the reader to the works by Martin Matustik, in particular *Postnational Identity: Critical Theory and Existential Philosophy in Habermas, Kierkegaard, and Havel* (New York and London: Guilford Press, 1993), and "Existence and the Communicatively Competent Self," *Philosophy and Social Criticism*, 25, 3 (1999), 93–120.

82 See Jürgen Habermas, *Philosophical-Political Profiles*, trans. Frederick G. Lawrence (Cambridge, MA: MIT Press, 1983), 199–211.

83 Interestingly, Habermas' assessment of Scholem's stand toward the secularization of religion is not unlike that developed by Theodor Adorno; see the fascinating discussion of Scholem in a letter from Adorno to Benjamin, from March 4, 1938, in Adorno and Benjamin, *The Complete Correspondence 1928–1940*, 249–50.

84 Johannes Baptist Metz has since taken up the challenge, see the essays collected in *Por una cultura de la memoria*, presentación y epílogo de Reyes Mate (Barcelona: Anthropos Editorial, 1999). See also Johann-Baptist Metz and Jürgen Moltmann, *Faith and the Future: Essays on Theology, Solidarity, and Modernity* (Maryknoll: Orbis Books, 1995).

1

The German Idealism of the Jewish Philosophers

"The Jew can play a creative role in nothing at all that concerns German life, neither in what is good nor in what is evil." This statement by Ernst Jünger has outlived the anti-Semitism of the conservative revolutionaries in whose name it was written more than a generation ago. I heard the identical assertion just a few years ago in the philosophy department of one of our great universities. As this version had it, Jews at best attain stardom of the second rank. At that time, when I was a student, I did not give it a second thought; I must have been occupied with reading Husserl, Wittgenstein, Scheler, and Simmel without realizing the descent of these scholars. However, the well-known philosophy professor who gainsaid the productivity of his Jewish colleagues did know of their origins. The stubbornness of the components of an ideology whose discrepancies could be conveyed by any lexicon is remarkable. If it were a matter of dissecting into pieces a form of the spirit such as that of German philosophy in the twentieth century, separating it out according to its parts, and putting it on the scales, then we would find in the domain supposedly reserved for German profundity a preponderance of those the same prejudice wants to assign to the outer court as merely critical talents.

It is not my intention here to offer another proof of what has long since been demonstrated. There is another situation much more in need of clarification: It remains astonishing how productively central motifs of the philosophy of German Idealism shaped so essentially by Protestantism can be developed in terms of the experience of the Jewish tradition. Because the legacy of the Kabbalah already flowed into and was absorbed by Idealism, its light seems to refract all the more richly in the spectrum of a spirit in which something of the spirit of Jewish mysticism lives on, in however hidden a way.

The abysmal and yet fertile relationship of the Jews with German philosophy shares in the social fate that once forced open the gates of the ghettos, for assimilation or reception of the Jews into bourgeois society became a reality only for the minority of Jewish intellectuals. Despite a century and a half of progressive emancipation, the broad mass of the Jewish people had not gotten beyond the formal aspects of equal rights. On the other hand, even the courtly Jews, like their successors, the Jewish bankers of the state of the nineteenth century, never became fully acceptable socially. Indeed, they had not striven so seriously to break down the barriers of their invisible ghetto; a universal emancipation would have threatened what privileges they possessed. Assimilation stretched only a thin protective layer around the permanently foreign body of Jewry. Its medium was a culture gained academically, its seal a baptism often socially coerced. If these cultivated Jews would give back to the culture intellectually as much as they owed to it, their social standing remained so ambivalent right into the 1920s that Ernst Jünger could not only deprecate their productivity as the "feuilleton prattle of civilization" but also put in question the process of assimilation: "To the same extent that the German will gains in sharpness and shape, it becomes increasingly impossible for the Jews to entertain even the slightest delusion that they can be Germans in Germany; they are faced with their final alternatives, which are, in Germany, either to be Jewish or not to be." This was in 1930, when those who could not adapt to a dubious politics of *apartheid* were already being offered the menacing promise that was so gruesomely kept in the concentration camps.

And so, precisely out of the marginal strata that had been assimilated most successfully, there emerged the spokesmen for a turning back of the German Jews to the origins of their own tradition. This movement found its political expression in Zionism and its philosophic expression in the (as it were, anticipated) existentialism of Martin Buber, who fastened onto the last phase of Jewish mysticism. The Polish and Ukrainian Hassidism of the eighteenth century had drawn its ideas from kabbalist writings, but the doctrine had retreated so far behind the personality of the Hassidic holy men that the traditionally idealized figure of the learned rabbi was pushed out by that of the folkish Zaddik, whose existence was the Torah become entirely and utterly living. In Buber's zeal against the rationalistically stulti-fied teaching of the rabbis and his appropriation of the religion of the people, which was full of mythic legends and mystical faces, a new pathos of existential philosophizing was enflamed:

> With the destruction of the Jewish communal spirit the fruitfulness of the spiritual conflict became weakened. Spiritual force is mustered henceforth on behalf of the preservation of the people against outside influences; the strict enclosure of one's own realm, to protect against penetration by alien tendencies; the codification of values in order to fend off every shift in values; the unmistakable, unreinter-pretable, hence consistently rational formulation of religion. In place of the God-filled, demanding, creative element there entered the ever more rigid, merely preserving, merely continuing, merely defen-sive element of official Judaism; indeed, it was directed ever more against the creative element, which seemed to endanger the status quo of the people by its audacity and freedom; it became its persecutor and life-enemy.

The Hassidic impulse first found a philosophical language in the work of Franz Rosenzweig. Rosenzweig, who with Buber translated the Bible into German, had worked on Hegel's philosophy of state as a student of Friedrich Meinecke. In his own great project he attempted – as the title of the three-volume work, *Star of Redemp-tion*, announced from afar – an interpretation of Idealist thought out of the depths of Jewish mysticism. Not only was he one of the first to establish links with Kierkegaard; he also took up motifs of the so-called late Idealism, especially from Schelling's last philosophy; thus he divulged the lineage of existentialist philosophy decades before it was painstakingly rediscovered by the official history of philosophy. The basic question on which the Idealist self-confidence in the power of the concept shatters is this: "How can the world be contingent, although it still has to be thought of as necessary?" Thought labors in vain on the impenetrable fact that things are so and not otherwise, that the historical existence of human beings is so profoundly bathed in enigmatic arbitrariness:

> Inasmuch as philosophy . . . denies this opaque presupposition of all life; that is, inasmuch as it does not let it hold good as something real but makes it into nothing, it conjures up for itself the illusion of

presuppositionlessness. . . . If philosophy wanted not to stop up its ears in the face of the cry of anguished humanity, it would have to start from this: that the nothingness of death is a something; that each new nothingness of death, as a new newly fruitful something, is not to be talked or written away. . . . Nothingness is not nothing, it is something. . . . We do not want a philosophy that deceives us by the all-or-nothing tone of its dance about the lasting domination of death. We want no deception.

The deception that has been seen through leads to the insight that the world, in which there is still laughter and crying, is itself caught up in becoming – the appearances still seek their essence. In the visible happening of nature is disclosed the growth of an invisible realm in which God himself looks forward to his redemption: "God, in the redemption of the world by human beings and of human beings in relation to the world, redeems himself."

Idealism only entered into competition with the theology of creation; still in bondage to Greek philosophy, it did not look upon the unreconciled world from the standpoint of possible redemption. Its logic remained in the grips of the past: "True lastingness is constantly in the future. Not what always was is lasting; not what gets renewed at all times, but solely what is to come: the kingdom." The meaning of this, of course, is only disclosed to a logic that does not, like that of Idealism, deny its linguistic body; it has to open itself up to the underlying logic deposited in the language – a resonance from the ancient kabbalist idea that language reaches God because it is sent out from God. Idealism condemned language as the instrument of knowledge and elevated a divinized art as its substitute. A Jew actually anticipated Heidegger, the *philosophicus teutonicus*, in this peculiarly heightened awareness.

Toward the end of World War I, Rosenzweig sent home the manuscript of *Star of Redemption* by mail from the field of battle. The way he conceived of the messianic vocation of Jewish exile during his time on the Balkan front is documented by a passage from one of his letters: "Because the Jewish people already stands beyond the opposition that forms the authentically dynamic power in the life of the nations, beyond the polarity of particularity and world history, of home and faith, of earth and heaven, so, too, it does not know war."

Another Jewish philosopher, Hermann Cohen, had on Christmas Day 1914 testified in the same sense to the students withdrawing from their studies to the field of battle that the political expression of the messianic idea is eternal peace: "Since the prophets as international politicians recognized evil as existing neither exclusively nor especially in individuals but in the nations instead, so the disappearance of war, eternal peace among the nations, became for them the symbol of morality on earth." Cohen, who so idiosyncratically takes Kant's idea of eternal peace back into the Old Testament, stands, however, in a different camp than Buber or Rosenzweig. He represents the liberal tradition of Jewish intellectuals who were inwardly connected with the German Enlightenment and supposed that in their spirit they might be capable of feeling at one with the nation in general. Immediately after the outbreak of the war, Cohen delivered before the Kant Society of Berlin a remarkable speech ("On the Peculiarity of the German Spirit") in which he exhibited to the imperialistic Germany of Wilhelm II and his military forces the original testimony of German humanism. Indignantly he dissociated himself from the "insulting" distinction between the nation of poets and thinkers and that of fighters and state builders: "Germany is and remains in continuity with the eighteenth century and its cosmopolitan humanity."

Less cosmopolitan is the tone of his apologia: "in us there struggles the originality of a nation with which no other can compare." This kind of loyalty to the state later delivered over those who in deluded pride called themselves National German Jews to the tragic irony of an identification with their attackers.

Cohen was the head of the famous Marburg School, in which there flowed the Jewish erudition of a generation that philosophized in the spirit of Kant and transformed Kant's teachings into an epistemology of natural science. Kant (who, after all, was so amazed at the linguistic power of Moses Mendelssohn that he once stated that "if the muse of philosophy should choose a language, she would choose this one") likewise selected, as a partner in the academic disputation concerning his *Habilitationsschrift*, a Jew: the onetime physician Marcus Herz. Just as Lazarus Bendavid had done in Vienna, in Berlin Herz put his all into propagating Kantian philosophy. The first one to go beyond promulgation to appropriate the new criticism in a productive way, and to push it radically beyond its own presuppositions was the genial Salomon Maimon, who had been inspired in his youth by Spinoza. Maimon went from being a beggar and vagrant to being a scholar protected by a patron; Fichte, who was not the least bit modest, conceded superiority to him without envy. Maimon, as Fichte wrote to Reinhold, has revolutionized Kantian philosophy from the ground up "without anyone's noticing." "I believe," continued Fichte, "future centuries will bitterly mock ours." German historians have not taken any impulse from this. This first generation of Jewish Kantians entered into oblivion, as did Kant in general.

It was the polemical writing of another Jew – the cry of Otto Liebmann that "there must be a return to Kant!" – that paved the way for a second Kantianism. Cohen was able to return to the matrix of problems prepared by Maimon. Cohen's great student Ernst Cassirer summarized his teacher's intention at Cohen's grave: "The primacy of activity over possibility, of the independent-spiritual over the sensible-thinglike, should be carried through purely and completely. Any appeal to a merely given should fall aside; in place of every supposed foundation in things there should enter the pure foundations of thinking, of willing, of artistic and religious consciousness. In this way, Cohen's logic became the logic of the origin."

Besides the direct "Marburg line," however, Arthur Liebert, Richard Honigswald, Emil Lask, and Jonas Cohn played a decisive role in the Kantian-tinted epistemology of the turn of the century. Moreover, Max Adler and Otto Bauer developed a Kantian version of Marxism. In this climate there was an exuberant development of the acuity in commentary and analysis that is ambiguously ascribed to the Jews as a natural quality – and that even Martin Buber suspects of a "dissociated spirituality," "a spirituality dissociated from the matrix of natural living and from the functions of a genuine spiritual conflict, neutral, insubstantial, dialectical, that could give itself to all objects, even the most indifferent, in order to dissect them conceptually or to place them in reciprocal relationships, also without really belonging in an intuitive-instinctual way to any one of them."

Now, it may be that the theories of knowledge and science that considered themselves to be without history and presuppositions did in fact appeal to the inclinations of those Jews who once had to achieve freedom of thought by renouncing tradition. The attachment of the generations brought up in the ghetto to the condition of an enlightened culture was purchased with a break from age-old obligation, a leap into a foreign history; for example, Mendelssohn had to keep his work with German literature secret from his fellow Jews! Perhaps the physiognomy of Jewish thought was also shaped by the fact that something of the distance characteristic of an originally foreign gaze had been preserved in it. Just as once-familiar things are more naked to an emigrant who has returned home after a long time, so a peculiar sharpness of vision is characteristic of one who has become assimilated. Because he lacks intimacy with the cultural realities that have been cooled down for his appropriation, they relinquish their structures to him all the more easily.

On the other hand, the rabbinic and especially the kabbalistic hermeneutics of the Holy Scriptures had schooled Jewish thought for centuries in the exegetical virtues of commentary and analysis, and the Jewish mind was drawn whenever possible by epistemology because its method gave a rationalized shape to its long-since customary mystical problematic. The mystic obtains the stages of the theogony, the developmental history of the coming to be of the Godhead, by turning the path of his soul toward God; consequently, his knowledge is always mediated by transcendental reflection on the mode of his own experience. It is no accident that Simmel's introduction to philosophy uses the mysticism of Meister Eckhart as the key to Kant's Copernican turn.

Kant's attractiveness to the Jewish mind is naturally to be explained first of all by the way he unfolded the free attitude of criticism based on rational belief and of cosmopolitan humanity into its most clairvoyant and authentic shape (aside from Goethe). Kant's humanism influenced the convivial social interchange – assimilation without insult – that had its moment in the salons of Berlin around the turn of the nineteenth century. What is more, critique was also the means of Jewish emancipation from Judaism itself. It not only secured an urbane attitude and worldly tolerance on the part of Christians; it also offered the philosophical tool with which the grand self-dynamism of the Jewish spirit sought to master its religious and social destiny. Jewish philosophy, in all its versions, has remained critique.

Society does not permit emancipation without a break. Because assimilation assumed forms of submission, many assimilated Jews became all the more Jewish in their private lives as a rigorous identification with the expectations of their environment allowed less and less room for them to present themselves publicly as anything other than emphatically German. This tension, so transparent from a social-psychological point of view, emerges from a posthumous work of Cohen dedicated to the memory of his Orthodox father, "Religion of Reason from the Sources of Judaism." The Kantian rationalism of the

Marburg School stripped away the specific pathos it owed to its Lutheran lineage; the theory was, so to speak, secularized again. But finally the layer of "civilization" to which the *Zivilisationsjuden* (as they were called) seemed so completely to have given themselves over broke open, and the question of the bindingness of the Mosaic Word of God pushed the aged Cohen to the margins of his system. Insofar as the humanity of nations had grown to the amplitude of a culture purified by philosophy and science, they surely shared the same religion of reason. However, the concept of reason, pictured in the image of a primordial spring, was illumined for the first time in history by the testimonies of the Jewish prophets. With utter rigor Cohen sought to salvage the autonomy of reason in relation to the positive nature of revelation. His philosophical conscience came to rest at last with the following tortuous notions: "If I am dependent upon the literary sources of the prophets for the concept of religion, so too would these remain mute and blind if I did not – under their tutelage, to be sure, but not just guided by their authority – approach them with a concept which I made the basis of my learning from them."

Of course, present-day theory of knowledge and science has not been determined by Cohen but by two other Jewish scholars. Inside Germany the phenomenology of Edmund Husserl and internationally the logical positivism inaugurated by Ludwig Wittgenstein have become predominant in this period.

In the year of Hermann Cohen's death, Wittgenstein's *Tractatus Logico-Philosophicus* appeared, opening with the lapidary statement "The world is everything that is the case." Wittgenstein was a major influence on the Vienna Circle, in which the Jews Otto Neurath and Friedrich Waismann were prominent. Later on, Jewish emigrants contributed to the worldwide triumph of the new doctrine. In the United States, Hans Reichenbach was the main influence; in Great Britain, Wittgenstein himself. At Cambridge, Wittgenstein led the life of a reclusive *Privatdozent*. Without publishing anything, and in the quiet of his colloquia with a small circle of students, he brought about the turn from logical to linguistic analysis. The chief concern of linguistic analysis was no longer with the analysis and step-by-step construction of a universal language that would picture facts. It did not serve a systematic purpose but rather a therapeutic one of explaining any given formulations by means of language analysis and expressing their meaning in "perfect clarity." Philosophical responses were confined to recommendations of this or that mode of expression and ended in the artistry of language games that found satisfaction exclusively in themselves.

After two and a half decades of silence and shortly before his death, Wittgenstein gave in to the urgings of his friends and students and allowed a second book, *Philosophical Investigations*, to appear. He added a foreword full of resignation: "Up to a short time ago I had really given up the idea of publishing my works in my lifetime. . . . I make them public with doubtful feelings. It is not impossible that it should fall to the lot of this work, in its poverty and in the darkness of this time, to bring light into one brain or another – but, of course, it is not likely." In *Philosophical Investigations* Wittgenstein extols as his authentic discovery one that makes us capable of breaking off philosophizing at any given place. Philosophy is supposed to come to rest, so that it can no longer get put in question by questioning itself. Already in the *Tractatus* his deeper impulses had been revealed in the following statement:

> We feel that, even when all possible questions have been answered, the problems of life remain completely untouched. Of course there are then no questions left, and this itself is the answer. The solution of the problem is seen in the vanishing of the problem. (Is this not the reason why those who have found after a long period of doubt that the sense of life became clear to them have then been unable to say what constituted that sense?)

Wittgenstein does not hesitate to apply this insight to his own reflections: "My propositions serve as elucidations in the following way: Anyone who understands them eventually recognizes them as nonsensical, when he has used them – as steps – to climb up beyond them. (He must, so to speak, throw away the ladder after he has climbed up to it.) . . . What we cannot speak about we must pass over in silence." Such a silence has a transitive meaning. Even what has been uttered must be taken back again into the broken silence. Rosenzweig's remark that "there is nothing more Jewish in the deeper sense than an ultimate misgiving toward the power of the word and an inward trust in the power of silence!" reads like a comment on this. Because Hebrew is not the language of the assimilated Jew's everyday life but is removed from this as the sacred language, he is deprived of the ultimate and most obvious freedom from constraint in life, which is to say, in his torment, what it is that he suffers: "For this reason he cannot speak with his brother at all, with him the look conveys far better than the word. . . . Precisely in silence and in the silent sign of discourse does the Jew feel even his everyday speech to be at home in the sacred speech of his ceremonial hour."

The Kabbalah differs from many other mystical writings in its complete lack of autobiography. Gershom Scholem, the historian of Jewish mysticism, reports that the kabbalists were bound to silence or to oral tradition; most manuscripts were abolished, and few of those that were still extant reached print. Seen from this vantage, Wittgenstein's use of language in speaking about the mystical appears thoroughly consistent: "There are, indeed, things that cannot be put into words. They make themselves manifest. They are what is mystical."

In contrast, Husserl sought to ground philosophy as an exact science precisely on the basis of a rigorous description of phenomena that make themselves manifest "by themselves" and are "given" intuitively in unmediated evidence. Transcendental phenomenology shares its intent with logical positivism, but not its path. Both fasten on the Cartesian starting point of doubt that never despairs of itself; however, the things [*Sachen*] to which Husserl would penetrate are not semantically and syntactically analyzable sentences of natural or scientific languages but achievements of consciousness out of which the meaningful network of our life world is constructed. Husserl did not wish to derive these intentions and their fulfillments, but simply to let them be seen from their "ultimate conceivable experiential standpoint"; in this he distinguished himself sharply from the Neo-Kantians and from the older Idealism in general. One day Plessner accompanied his teacher Husserl home after a seminar; he recalls the following: "When we reached his garden gate his deeper displeasure erupted: 'I have always found German Idealism in its entirety disgusting. All my life I' – and here he drew up his slender walking stick with the silver handle and pressed it against the gateposts – 'have sought reality.' In an unsurpassably plastic way the walking stick portrayed the intentional act and the post its fulfillment."

Husserl was isolated in his Freiburg home as the political horizon began to cloud over. He could lecture publicly about his mature philosophy only outside Germany, in Vienna and Prague. Unlike Wittgenstein, he did not withdraw the systematic claim into the self-complacency of linguistic glass-bead games or into the stillness of the mystically unspeakable. Instead he attempted a great final project that was supposed to apprehend the crisis of the European sciences as the crisis of European humanity and to overcome it. Against the waves of fascist irrationalism, Husserl wanted to erect the claim of a renewed rationalism: "The reason for the failure of a rational culture . . . lies not in the essence of rationalism itself but solely in its being rendered superficial, in its entanglement in 'naturalism' and 'objectivism.'" In a genuinely Idealist fashion, he believed he could head off the disaster if only he could successfully ground the *Geisteswissenschaften* in a phenomenologically exact way. The crisis seemed to be rooted precisely in that a rationalism rendered superficial sought its grounding in a false and perilous way, by a natural scientific reduction of all spiritual phenomena to their physically explainable substructures. Instead of this, Husserl believed that the spirit should climb back into itself and clarify the achievements of consciousness hitherto hidden to itself. Husserl placed his trust in the world-moving force of this "theoretical attitude": ". . . this is not only a new cognitive stance. Because of the requirement to subject all empirical matters to ideal norms, i.e., those of unconditioned truth, there soon results a far-reaching transformation of the whole praxis of human existence, i.e., the whole of cultural life."

Though he had a rather questionable way of phrasing it, Husserl would have liked to bestow on philosophers the vocation of "functionaries of humanity." In his earlier works he had worked out the procedures through which phenomenologists would be assured a correct cognitive attitude. A kind of derealizing of reality was supposed to dissolve their interested involvement in the process of real life in order to make pure theory possible. In this withdrawn state, which he called *epoche*, Husserl daily exercised an admirable asceticism. He meditated for months and years, and from the written reports of his meditations grew the mountains of posthumous research manuscripts – documents of a working philosophy neither lectured on nor published. What Husserl practiced, then, was a methodological exercise. When politics drew him away from contemplation, however, the old philosopher attributed to it a bearing on the philosophy of history. The theory that grew out of a withdrawal from all praxis was supposed in the end to make possible the "new sort of praxis" of a politics directed by science – "a praxis whose aim is to elevate mankind through universal scientific reason according to norms of truth of all forms, to transform it from the bottom up into a new humanity made capable of an absolute self-responsibility on the basis of absolute theoretical insights."

This little mantle of philosophy of history was already threadbare before Husserl drew it over his doctrine, which was unhistorical to the core. Still he persisted in his stance; he fought for his lost cause with pathos and with the illusion of pure theory.

How much this cause was lost became evident in 1929 in the famous dispute between Cassirer and Heidegger in Davos. The theme was Kant, but in truth the end of an epoch was up for discussion. The opposition of the schools paled beside that of the generations. Cassirer represented the world to which Husserl belonged against his great pupil – the cultivated world of European humanism against a decisionism that invoked the primordiality of thought, whose radicality attacked the Goethe culture at its very roots.

It is no accident that the Goethe cult at the start of the nineteenth century was created in the salon of Rachel Varnhagen, for it is certain that no one else strove with such intensity to live in accord with the model of Wilhelm Meister, who understood the "cultivation of personality" so peculiarly and so deceptively as an assimilation of the bourgeois to the nobleman, as did those Jews who were also called "exceptional Jews of culture." What they expected of that model has been expressed by Simmel: "Perhaps no one has lived as symbolic a life as Goethe, since he gave to each only a piece or facet of his personality and yet at the same gave 'the whole to everyone.' To live symbolically in this manner is the only possibility of not being a comedian and a role player." The interiorized Goethe promised not only the way to assimilation, but also the solution to the Jews' ordeal of constantly having to play a role without being capable of being identical with oneself. In this twofold respect, the culture of German classicism was socially necessary for the Jews. Perhaps it is precisely for this reason that we owe to them the most sensitive aesthetic reflections, from Rosenkranz and Simmel, through Benjamin and Lukács, down to Adorno.

In the course of the conversations at Davos, a student put three questions to Cassirer; each of his responses closed with a Goethe citation. Heidegger, however, polemicized against the flaccid aspect of a human being who merely made use of the works of the spirit; Heidegger wanted "to cast [things] back upon the toughness of fate." The discussion came to an end with Heidegger's refusal to take Cassirer's outstretched hand. What Heidegger announced four years

later, at the Leipzig election rally of German scientists in the name
of Hitler's party, reads today like a continuation of these events:

> We have broken with the idolization of a thinking without grounding
> and power. We are seeing the end of a philosophy capable of serving
> it. . . . The primordial courage in the confrontation with what is –
> either to grow from it or to be shattered by it – is the innermost moti-
> vation behind the inquiry of a science rooted in a national people
> (*völkischen Wissenschaft*). For courage lets us go forward; courage
> releases us from what has held true up to now; courage risks the unac-
> customed and the incalculable.

It was this incalculable factor that Cassirer had at that very moment
to escape. Emigration led him to the United States by way of Sweden
and England. There he wrote his final work, *Myth of the State*, whose
closing chapter deals with the technique of modern political myths
and ends with a commentary on a Babylonian legend: "The world of
human culture could not arise before the darkness of myth was van-
quished and overcome. But the mythical monsters were not defini-
tively destroyed."

Heidegger's questionable victory over the humanitarian intellec-
tuality of Cassirer takes on a special inexorability from the fact
that he convicted the enlightened position of a real weakness as
well: In the face of the thought now proclaimed as "radical," the
roots of the eighteenth century do not reach sufficiently deep. Before
the eighteenth century there was no Jewish West, only the Middle
Ages of the ghetto. A return to the Greeks, whenever it was
attempted by Jews, always had about it something of a lack in power.
Power secretly resided only in the depths of their own tradition, the
Kabbalah.

Over the centuries the kabbalists had elaborated the technique
of allegorical interpretation, before Walter Benjamin rediscovered
allegory as the key to knowledge. Allegory is the counternotion of
symbol. Cassirer had conceived every content of myth, philosophy,
art, and language as the world of symbolic forms. In that world's
objective spirit, human beings communicated with one another, and
in it alone were they able to exist at all, for in the symbolic form –
as Cassirer believed himself capable of saying with Goethe – the
inconceivable is wrought, the ineffable is brought to speech, and the
essence is brought to appearance. But Benjamin recalled that history

– in all that it contains from the outset of the untimely, the painful, the failed – is shut off from expression through the symbol and from the harmony of the classical pattern. Only allegorical representation succeeds in portraying world history as a history of suffering. Allegories are in the realm of thoughts what ruins are in the realm of things: "To preserve the unfreedom, imperfection, and brokenness of the sensible, the beautiful physis, was essentially denied to classicism. Precisely this, however, the allegories of the baroque, hidden beneath their bold pomp, bring out with hitherto unanticipated emphasis."

Before the gaze schooled in allegory the innocence of a philosophy of symbolic forms is lost; before it is disclosed the fragility of that foundation – firmly and conclusively established, so it seemed, by Kant and Goethe – of an enlightened culture of beauty. It was not as though Benjamin had given up its idea, but he saw in its roots the schizoid nature of precisely those "cultural values" and "cultural treasures" that Jews were discussing so naively. In truth, history was the triumphal procession of the rulers over those lying on the ground: "According to traditional practice, the spoils are carried along in the procession. They are called cultural treasures. . . . There is no document of civilization that is not at the same time a document of barbarism. And just as such a document is not free of barbarism, barbarism taints also the manner in which it was transmitted from one owner to the other" (Benjamin, *Illuminations* (New York, 1969), p. 256).

Benjamin took his own life in 1940 when, after his flight through southern France, the Spanish border officials threatened to deliver him over to the Gestapo. The theses on the philosophy of history that he left behind are among the most moving testimonies of the Jewish spirit. In it the dialectic of the Enlightenment, which in its broken progress dominates the as yet undecided course of history, is held fast in the form of an allegorical interpretation. The ninth thesis says

A Klee painting named "Angelus Novus" shows an angel looking as though he is about to move away from something he is fixedly contemplating. His eyes are staring, his mouth is open, his wings are spread. This is how one pictures the angel of history. His face is turned toward the past. Where we perceive a chain of events, he sees one single catastrophe which keeps piling wreckage upon wreckage and hurls it in front of his feet. The angel would like to stay, awaken the dead, and make whole what has been smashed. But a storm is blowing from paradise; it has got caught in his wings with such violence that the angel can no longer close them. This storm irresistibly propels him into the future to which his back is turned, while the pile of debris before him grows skyward. This storm is what we call progress. (*Illuminations*, pp. 257–8)

Benjamin was not the first to break through the circle of Jewish thought devoted to the theory of science and to epistemology, which later was expanded to encompass the philosophy of history. Already Simmel, who had been a friend of George and Rilke as much as of Bergson and Rodin, had crossed the boundaries of the then dominant academic philosophy: "There are three categories of philosophers: one group hears the heartbeat of things, a second only that of human beings, a third only that of concepts; . . . [the philosophy professors] hear only the heart of the literature."

In Simmel's posthumous writings there is a characteristic fragment on the art of the drama that deals with an experience that often lends a nervous dynamism to the private lives of assimilated Jews. Hannah Arendt, the clever historian of anti-Semitism, has described how the philo-Semitic circles in *fin de siècle* Paris accepted cultivated Jews with the curious compliment that one could no longer even tell their descent; they were supposed to be Jews, but not be like Jews:

In this ambiguous back and forth each of the individuals in question was an accomplished actor; it was only that the curtain that should have normally brought the play to an end would never again be lowered and the people who had made a theatrical role out of their entire lives no longer knew who they really were, even in solitude. If they entered into society, they instinctively detected those who were like them; they recognized one another automatically from the unusual mixture of arrogance and anxiety that had determined and fixed each of their gestures. Out of this there arose the knowing smile of the clique – which Proust discussed at such length – which . . . only indicated secretly what everyone else present had long known, namely that in every corner of the salon of Countess So-and-so there was sitting another Jew who was never allowed to admit it, and who without this in itself insignificant fact would oddly enough never have arrived in the much sought after corner.

On top of this, Jews who were held personally responsible for the pitilessness of their environment in terms of an "enigmatic demonism of mask changing" could not but become sensitive to the role character of human existence in general. If I bring one of Simmel's insights into connection with this sharpened sensibility, this does not bring its validity into doubt. It goes as follows:

> We not only do things to which culture and the blows of fate induce us from without, but we inevitably represent something that we really are not. . . . It is very seldom that a person determines his mode of behavior in complete purity out of his very own existence; usually we see a preexisting form before us which we have filled with our individual conduct. Now this: that the human being experiences, or represents a predesignated other as the development entrusted to him as most centrally his own, so that he does not simply abandon his own being, but fills the other with this being itself and guides its streams into those manifoldly divided arteries whose paths, though running a preset course, absorb the whole inner being into this particular shape – this is the pre-form [*Vorform*] of the art of theater. . . . In just this sense we are all somehow actors.

Helmut Plessner, too, developed his general anthropology out of his "anthropology of the actor." The human being does not merely live in the midst of his body, like the animal. Without being able to eliminate this centering, he also falls outside it; he constantly has to relate to himself and to others, to lead a self-enacted life in accord with the "director's instructions" of the society:

> As a relation-to-himself the actor is the person of a role, for himself and for the spectator. In accord with this relationship the players and spectators only repeat, however, the distancing of people from themselves and one another that pervades their daily life. . . . For what is this seriousness of everydayness in the end but realizing-oneself-bound-to-a-role which we want to play in society? To be sure, this role-playing does not want to be a performance. . . . the burden of image-projecting for our social role is taken from us by the tradition into which we were born. Nonetheless, we, as virtual spectators of ourselves and the world, have to see the world as a stage.

An anthropology that apprehends the human in terms of his compulsion to play a role finds its continuation without any break whatsoever in sociology. Simmel, like Plessner, worked in a sociological mode; so, too, did Max Scheler, the real founder of philosophical anthropology. During his last years, Scheler taught sociology at the University of Frankfurt, which had gained fame, in virtue of the influence of Franz Oppenheimer, Gottfried Salomon, Carl Grünberg, and Karl Mannheim, as a center of sociological research. There Max Horkheimer united his chair in philosophy with the directorship of the Institute for Social Research, and even Martin Buber became a sociologist.

The Jewish spirit dominated sociology from the days of Ludwig Gumplowicz on. The Jews' experience of society as something one runs up against was so insistent that they carried along a sociological view, so to speak, right from their doorsteps. In neighboring disciplines, too, it was they who were the first to employ a sociological point of view. Eugen Ehrlich and Hugo Sinzheimer founded the sociology of law. Ludwig Goldscheid and Herbert Sultan were the leading sociologists of finance.

The fantasy of Jewish scholars in general was sparked by the power of money – Marx, especially the young Marx, was an example of this. In this regard the intimate enmity of the cultured Jews toward the moneyed Jews – that sublime intra-Jewish anti-Semitism against the stratum whose *imago* was minted by the Rothschilds – might have been a motive. Simmel, himself the son of a salesman, wrote a blatant "Philosophy of Money." In Simmel, however, one also finds the other typically Jewish interest besides the sociological: the interest in a philosophy of nature inspired by mysticism. His diary includes this: ". . . treat not only each human but also each thing as if it were an end in itself that would result in a cosmic ethics." The mystical link between morality and physics is again encountered here, in Kantian terminology. Simmel's friend Karl Joel wrote about the "Origins of Philosophy of Nature from the Spirit of Mysticism." In the 1920s, David Baumgardt undertook to repair the so-called injustice done to Baader, whom a positivistic age had forgotten so completely. In Baumgardt's "Franz Baader and Philosophical Romanticism," a Jew comes across the golden vein of those speculations on the ages of the world – so pregnant for a philosophy of nature – that lead from Jacob Böhme via Swabian Pietism to the Tübingen seminarians Schelling, Hegel, and Hölderlin. Even before this, Richard Unger had recognized in Hamann's tension-filled relationship to the Enlightenment the "realistic strain" of Protestant mysticism, which, with its acceptance of a ground of nature in God, is differentiated from the spiritualistic mysticism of the Middle Ages.

Even Scheler's and Plessner's sketches of a philosophy of nature exhibit a certain strain of this tradition. Despite all their sober elaboration of materials from the particular sciences, they still betray a speculative bent that stems from nature mysticism; Scheler's cosmology even reverts explicitly to a God that becomes.

However, all these Jewish scholars seem not to have attained full awareness of what force had set them on the path of this special tradition. They had forgotten what was still generally known at the close of the seventeenth century. At that time Johann Jacob Spaeth, a disciple of Böhmean mysticism, overcome by the consonance of this doctrine with the theosophy of Isaac Luria, went over to Judaism. A few years later, the Protestant pastor Friedrich Christoph Oetinger (whose writings Hegel and Schelling as well as Baader had read) sought out in the ghetto of Frankfurt the kabbalist Koppel Hecht in order to be initiated into Jewish mysticism. Hecht responded that "Christians have a book that speaks about the Kabbalah more clearly than the Zohar;" what he meant was the work of Jacob Böhme.

It was this kind of "theology" Walter Benjamin had in mind when he remarked that historical materialism would have been able to accept motifs of kabbalistic mysticism without further ado if only it were capable of assuming theology into its service. This reception actually happened with Ernst Bloch. In the medium of his Marxian appropriation of Jewish mysticism, Bloch combines sociology with the philosophy of nature into a system that today is borne along as is no other by the great breath of German Idealism. In the summer of 1918 Bloch published *The Spirit of Utopia*, which holds up a Marxism confined to economics to a mirror. *The Spirit of Utopia* is comparable to a *Critique of Pure Reason* for which the *Critique of Practical Reason* still needed to be written. Bloch writes

> Here the economy is sublated; but what is missing is the soul, the faith
> for which room is to be made; the clever, active gaze has destroyed
> everything, to be sure, much that needed destroying. . . . Also it
> disavowed with good reason the all-too-arcadian socialism, the
> utopian-rationalist socialism that had reemerged since the Renaissance
> in the secularized guise of the Thousand-Year Reich, and often
> enough merely as a formless drapery, the ideology of very sober class
> goals and economic revolutions. But of course the utopian tendency
> is not adequately conceived in all this; nor is the substance of its wish

images met and judged; and the primordial religious desire is certainly not disposed of . . . being realized in a divine fashion, of finally installing ourselves chiliastically in the goodness, freedom, and light of the *telos*.

In Lurianic mysticism the idea is developed of the universe's arising in virtue of a process of shrinkage and contraction; God withdraws into an exile within himself. In this way the primordial impenetrability and power of matter is explained, as well as the positive character of evil, which can no longer be facilely evaporated into a shadow side of the good. On the other hand, this dark ground remains a nature in God; the nature of God remains a divine potency, the world soul or *natura naturans*. Into these depths reaches the notion Bloch lays at the basis of speculative materialism: Matter is in need of redemption. Since the time of that theological catastrophe described by the Zohar in the image of a shattering of a vessel, all things bear within themselves a break; they are, as Bloch expresses it, abstracted forms of themselves. The process of restoration was almost already completed when Adam's fall once again threw the world down from its proper stage and threw God back into exile. This new age of the world, with the ancient goal of the redemption of humanity, of nature, and indeed of the God knocked off his throne, is now the responsibility of humans. Mysticism becomes a magic of interiority, for now the outermost reality depends on what is most inward. (An old saying from the Zohar guarantees the redemption as soon as only a single community does perfect penance.) Prayer becomes a manipulative activity with significance for the philosophy of history.

For Bloch, political praxis replaces religious practice. The chapter "Marx, Death, and Apocalypse" also bears the subtitle "On the Way of the World, How What is Turned Inward Can Get Turned Outward." In this chapter is found the following statement:

> For ages matter has been an embarrassment not only for those seeking knowledge, but an embarrassment in itself; it is a demolished house within which the human being did not come forth; nature is a rubbish heap of deceived, dead, rotted, confused, and wasted life. . . . Only the good, thoughtful person holding the key can usher in the morning in this night of annihilation, if only those who remained impure do not weaken him, if only his crying for the Messiah is inspired enough to stir up the saving hands, to ensure for himself in a precise way the

grace of attainment, to arouse in God the forces drawing us and himself over, the inspiriting and grace-filled forces of the Sabbath reign, and thus to swallow up in victory the raw, satanic, breathtaking moment of conflagration of the apocalypse and straightaway to vanquish it.

Bloch's five-part work *The Principle of Hope* contains his clearest elucidation of this early vision and of its place in intellectual history. He has now sublated the Schelling of *Ages of the World* into the Marx of the *Paris Manuscripts*:

> Human abundance as well as that of nature as a whole . . . , the real genesis, is not at the beginning, but at the end; and it starts coming to be only when society and human existence become radical, that is, take hold of themselves at the roots. The root of history, however, is the toiling, laboring human being, who develops whatever has been given and transforms it. Once he has apprehended himself and grounded being without estrangement and alienation in real democracy, there thus arises in the world something that appears to everyone during childhood and yet within which no one ever was: home.

Because Bloch recurs to Schelling, and Schelling had brought from the spirit of Romanticism the heritage of the Kabbalah into the Protestant philosophy of German Idealism, the most Jewish elements of Bloch's philosophy – if such categories have any meaning at all – are at the same time the authentically German ones. They make a mockery of the attempt to draw such a distinction at all.

Just as Bloch (from the Schellingian spirit) and Plessner (from the Fichtean spirit) appropriated German Idealism and made good its prescient insights in relation to the present state of the sciences, so too it was Jewish scholars (friends of Walter Benjamin) who thought out Hegel's dialectic of the Enlightenment to a point where the ongoing beginning opens up a view of the still outstanding end: Theodor Adorno, Max Horkheimer, and Herbert Marcuse, preceded by the early Georg Lukács.

> I wrote this piece for a series of radio programs devoted to "Portraits from German-Jewish Intellectual History." Thilo Koch, to whose initiative the series must be credited, requested all contributors to record in concluding the experiences they had as authors during the course of working on their theme. My conclusion follows.

Wherever genuine philosophizing begins mere reportage comes to an end, and my task was only the latter. I had hesitations about undertaking it. Would not this undertaking – despite the high hopes with which it was planned – pin a Jewish star on the exiled and the beaten once again?

At the age of 15 or 16 I sat before the radio and experienced what was being discussed before the Nuremburg tribunal; when others, instead of being struck silent by the ghastliness, began to dispute the justice of the trial, procedural questions, and questions of jurisdiction, there was that first rupture, which still gapes. Certainly, it is only because I was still sensitive and easily offended that I did not close myself to the fact of collectively realized inhumanity in the same measure as the majority of my elders. For the same reason, the so-called Jewish question remained for me a very present past, but not itself something present. There was a clear barrier against the slightest hint of distinguishing Jews from non-Jews, Jewish from non-Jewish, even nominally. Although I had studied philosophy for years before I started on this study, I was not aware of the lineage of even half of the scholars named in it. Such naiveté is not adequate today, in my opinion.

Scarcely twenty-five years ago the cleverest and most important German theorist of state law – not just some Nazi, but Carl Schmitt himself – was capable of opening a scientific conference with the horrible statement that "we need to liberate the German spirit from all Jewish falsifications, falsifications of the concept of spirit which have made it possible for Jewish emigrants to label the great struggle of Gauleiter Julius Streicher as something unspiritual." At that time Hugo Sinzheimer responded from his exile in Holland with a book on the Jewish classics of German jurisprudence. In his conclusion, Sinzheimer turns his attention to this same Carl Schmitt:

> If one attends to the origins of the scholarly activity of the Jews at the time of the emancipation, it is not a matter of an influence of the Jewish spirit on German scientific labor. . . . Perhaps nowhere else in the world has the spiritual life of Germany celebrated greater triumphs outside its origins than precisely in this period when the ghetto was opened up and the intellectual powers of the Jews, held in check for so long, encountered what were the heights of the culture of Germany. It is the German spirit that lies at the basis of the Jewish influence.

To repeat this truth and to confirm it once again in connection with the fate of the Jewish philosophy is, of course, not unimportant, and yet it is still based on a question dictated by the opponent. Meanwhile the question of anti-Semitism itself has been disposed of – we have disposed of it by physical extermination. Hence, in our deliberations it cannot be a matter of the life and survival of the Jews, of influences back and forth; only we ourselves are at stake. That is to say, the Jewish heritage drawn from the German spirit has become indispensable for our own life and survival. At the very moment when German philosophers and scientists started to "eradicate" this heritage, the profound ambivalence that so eerily colored the dark ground of the German spirit was revealed as a danger of barbarism for everyone. Ernst Jünger, Martin Heidegger, and Carl Schmitt are representatives of this spirit in its grandeur, but in its perilousness as well; that they spoke as they did in 1930, 1933, and 1936 is no accident. And that this insight has not been realized a quarter of a century later proves the urgency of a discriminating kind of thinking all the more. This has to be one with that fatal German spirit and yet split with it from within to such an extent that it can relay an oracle to it: it must not cross the Rubicon a second time. If there were not extant a German-Jewish tradition, we would have to discover one for our own sakes. Well, it does exist; but because we have murdered or broken its bodily carriers, and because, in a climate of an unbinding reconciliation, we are in the process of letting everything be forgiven and forgotten too (in order to accomplish what could not have been accomplished better by anti-Semitism), we are now forced into the historical irony of taking up the Jewish question without the Jews.

The German Idealism of the Jews produces the ferment of a critical utopia. Its intention finds no more exact, more worthy, more beautiful expression than in the Kafkaesque passages at the end of Adorno's *Minima Moralia*:

> Philosophy, in the only way it is to be responsive in the face of despair, would be the attempt to treat all things as they would be displayed from the standpoint of redemption. Knowledge has no light but what shines on the world from the redemption; everything else is exhausted in reconstruction and remains a piece of technique. Perspectives would have to be produced in which the world is similarly displaced, estranged, reveals its tears and blemishes the way they once lay bare

as needy and distorted in the messianic light. To gain such a perspective without caprice and violence, utterly out of sympathy with the objects – this alone is worth the thinker's while. It is the simplest thing of all, because the situation cries out urgently for such knowledge, yes, because the completed negativity, once it is brought entirely into view, includes the mirror script of its opposite. But it is also something utterly impossible, because it presupposes a vantage point, even though it might concern a minute matter, which is removed from the range of human existence, whereas, of course, any possible knowledge does not have to be bullied merely by that which is in order to prove normative; but precisely for this reason it is itself fraught with the same distortion and neediness it intended to evade. The more passionately thought girds itself against its conditionedness for the sake of the unconditional, the less consciously and hence more perilously does it fall to the world. It even has to conceive its own impossibility for the sake of possibility. In relation to the exigency that thereby impinges upon it, the question about the reality or unreality of redemption itself is almost a matter of indifference.

Translated by Frederick G. Lawrence

2

On the Difficulty of Saying No

In the language of Roman trial law, "protest" had a strategic meaning: publicly breaking a silence that otherwise could have been misinterpreted as assent to a presented interpretation. The language of protest battles the suffocation in wordless conformity. The peculiar, deep conformism that has spread, cripplingly, in the Federal Republic has generated protest and, occasionally, a protestational form of thinking. It is directed against a form of indifference whose cause – whether an identification with everything and everyone, or a simple flight from identification altogether – is no longer discernible. Klaus Heinrich offers a commentary on the singular experience of this indifference in his *Essays on the Difficulty of Saying No.*[1]

These reflections on the complications of protest speech (which arise in cases of wrongly directed protest, as well as absent protest) do not rest on analyses of contemporary examples; they eschew the transparent biographical excuse, namely the difficulty of living as an intellectual in this Federal Republic. If this book still fell under a scientific or scholarly rubric, one could regard it as a critique of the false consciousness of ontology *and* of positivism. Heinrich philosophizes according to the rules of art, but the result of his artfulness is not in fact a philosophical undertaking.

Heinrich conceives of protest as opposition [*Widerspruch*] to processes of self-destruction. He has in mind those sublime forms of destruction that psychoanalysis has revealed in the intertwinement of individual life histories as well as in the fluctuations of collective states of consciousness – in other words, ruinings and self-destructions that do not relate directly to physical life. Heinrich does not focus on the risks of preserving material life, threatened economically in the impoverished regions of the world and politically and militarily even in the most highly developed ones. His concern is neither with nutritional capacities, nor with population explosion; neither with radiation damage and genetics, nor with the conditions for technological progress and economic growth; neither with the relation between strategies for national defense and global annihilation, nor with an internationalized civil war and the nuclear compulsion toward peaceful coexistence. The dimension of self-destruction that Heinrich puts up for discussion refers instead to a fact that that our positivist times would far prefer to deny: that the reproduction of the human species is assured only in the demanding form of historical survival. Socialized individuals can obviously only secure their existence via organized adaptive processes to the natural environment, and through readaptation to the social system of labor itself, to the extent that they mediate this metabolic interaction with nature through a highly precarious equilibrium of individuals with one another.

Material conditions for survival are therefore tightly interconnected with the most abstract conditions; the organic equilibrium is linked with another fragile balance between separation and unification, which engages the identity of each individual I through communication with others. The failed identity of the self-asserting I, like the failure of communication with the other speaker, are self-destructions that, in the end, have physical ramifications as well. These are perceptible as psychosomatic disturbances within the sphere of the individual. But shattered biographies also reflect the shattered reality of institutions. We know the painstaking process of continually renewing self-identification from Hegel's phenomenology of Spirit, as well as from Freud's psychoanalysis: the problem is one of an identity that can be constructed only through identifications, and this means precisely through renunciations [*Entäußerungen*] of identity. At the same time, this is the problem of a form of communication that allows a saving balance between speechless oneness and speechless alienation, between the sacrifice of individuality and the isolation of the abstractly individuated I. This balance must be achieved anew at each stage of development, and can fail at each stage as well. Experiences of the threatened loss of identity and the collapse of verbal communication are repeated over the course of every life history. But these are no less real than the collective experiences of species history, which the collective social subject undergoes in the course of the conflict with nature, as well as with itself.

Protest speech, whose difficulties Heinrich investigates, is directed against subterranean processes of self-destruction within society – a society which, in its present state of development, and with the dangers of reification on the one side and amorphousness on the other, must allow its members to form their fragile identities, and to sustain them within the nonidentity of successful communication. Claims about the maturity of the individual are simultaneously claims about the autonomy of society as well:

> The I-Self is never either itself or not-itself; neither identity nor non-identity, rather only the construction of an identity of both. Saying no, speaking out against the diremption [*Zerreissung*] between these two, is the first word of language. Yet it directs itself not only against diremption but also against a dirempted reality. And it searches within that reality for models of balance. It needs an opposed other [*Gegenüber*], on which it can support itself – and against which it can set itself.

The two central chapters of the book describe the difficulty of protesting against the self-destruction of a society as it sinks into indifference; the problem of identity under the threat of a loss of identity; and the problem of communication in a state of habitual-ized speechlessness.

Since time immemorial humans have interpreted crises of inner equilibrium through myths, religions, and philosophies, which testify to the experiences of the painstaking formation of the subject of a species history. A theologian by training, Heinrich is thus able to interpret the most contemporary affects by freely referring to the oldest of traditions. In the world religions, he uncovers a variety of models for a "durable identification," and in this way arrives at a surprising interpretation of the constitution of identity, on whose basis Fichte had already set the dialectical philosophy of identity into motion. This time, of course, dialectics is conceived as verbal communication, which the Socratic reciprocity of unforced dialogue between autonomous human beings must wrest from a repressive natural history. In situations of the domination of not yet realized mature autonomy [*Mündigkeit*], dialectics is the counter-offensive against the suppression of dialogue. Protest – saying no – is, in the end, the demand to think dialectically.

Heinrich develops this claim of the dialectic – and here we find the real philosophical intention of the work – in opposition to the claims of ontological thought, which, rather than revealing and over-coming the powers of origin that threaten humanity with destruc-tion, merely repress them. Ontology appears as a failed attempt to transmute the positivity of threatened non-being into the simple negation of a purified Being, of authenticity separated from all that is inauthentic; of the true, right, and certain scrupulously separated out from the false, the evil, and the perilous. Of course, in this manner ontology only cloaks a contradictory reality. Against Parmenides, Heinrich raises the claim of dialectical thinking from the Old Testament *topos* of communal fellowship [*Bundesgenossenschaft*]. Unlike the Greek philosophers, the prophets of Israel did not con-ceive of the life-giving, life-preserving context as a sphere of blessed unity of all forms of life, elevated above all that is nihilating, tran-sient, and illusory within one originary, complete Being – not as *cosmos*, that is – but instead as a universal bond whose power can only prove itself in the communication of traitors throughout the history of socialized humanity. Even in betrayal, a collectivity holds the fragmented world together, namely as the context of guilt. As long as this is not suppressed as a context of guilt, and remains a moving force, it clings to justice, to the idea of blessed unity, even if only as its mirror image. In this tradition – which seeks in all that has died out the traces of the still living, in all that is shattered the traces of unity – the place that ontology allots to the "forgetfulness of Being" is replaced by a different category: self-destructive betrayal. This betrayal, deceiving even the traitor himself that it is he who ulti-mately betrays and sells himself, is presented in two figures: as the loss of identity, which dissolves the I that had formed in and through the world, and as the breakdown of communication, which does not so much permit the speaker to lapse into silence as strike him dumb.

Unlike ontology, the critique of these representations of the untrue life (which are no longer conscious of their own untruth) does not orient itself in terms of a Being purified of non-being, or an authen-ticity that demands participation and obedience. Critique now does not return to the origins of the powers threatening humanity with the loss of I and of speech; it seeks rather to break that power, to "escape from the origin," and with the attainment of an I born out of conflict, to avert the danger which annihilates the continuity of history and pulls historical life into chaos, in individual neuroses no

less than in collective catastrophes. Wherever individual consciousness is able to find and maintain its balance between fusion and isolation, the communication between speakers is the only power in
which the powers of the origin can be mastered. It is this power to
which subjects owe their "mature *autonomy*" [*Mündigkeit*].

Heinrich himself formulates his thesis in this way:

> We know of two responses to the threat of an uncertain fate. One, in
> its renunciation of the world, seeks to overcome the world's ambigu-
> ous embodiments and, faced with the vision of an eternal fate, seeks
> to make itself one with that fate. The other, faced with a world of
> ambiguous embodiments, recognizes and assumes the struggle against
> the ambiguity of the world as its own fate. The first response is given
> by the philosophers of Greece; the second by the prophets of Israel.
> While the first response rebels against the ambiguous embodiments of
> the world, nevertheless remaining unable to save its own "arrogance"
> (the philosophical counterpart to the hubris of the tragic heroes) from
> "repentance," the other breaks the power of domination of expanded
> space and accelerated time. In its struggle against Baal, it protests
> against the unbroken powers of origin. And against those powers, it
> opposes the one power which, in distorted form, is also within it.

Against the ontological illusion of pure theory, the dialectician
opposes a knowledge that, beyond its very interests, finally fulfills its
intention.

Protest as advocacy for an achieved identity and successful
communication is dialectics; indeed dialectics consists precisely in
saying no (whose difficulties Heinrich analyzes) because in the
redeemed context of life the demonic powers themselves would
have to pass away, and could not be negated in favor of some
distinctive region of pure unity: the power of the redeeming word
must be wrested from the demonic powers themselves, to which they
then are forfeit. The traitors can and must be shown that it is they
themselves whom they betray. Protest wins its strength only to the
degree that it first identifies with those against whom it protests. In
this sense, the trickster is interpreted as a conformist who, through
pointed collaboration, sheds light on a reality beyond conformism.
The techniques of this cunning form of resistance are also depicted
in the story of Odysseus, and in the work of the supremely cunning
Brecht, above all in the inversions of the animal fables and the *Three-
penny Opera*.

Heinrich's perspective, in the end, reveals the affinity of ontological and positivist consciousnesses. Both collapse into the suggestive illusion of pure theory; both share the intention of using abstract distinctions to rid the world of the demons it fears. Whether reason elevates itself into a static contemplation of the eternal, or reduces itself to an instrument for the processing of the ready-to-hand, both ontology and positivism remain equally helpless against the return of repressed powers. The ascent to the indifferent power of origin of the one, unutterable Being renders resistance and the language of protest just as incapable of reflection as the exorcism of all empiristically meaningless statements under the compulsion of restricted forms of experience. The last version of Heidegger's ontology is the reverse side of the same coin that positivism had stamped with the seal of speechlessness. This ontology fetishizes words, bows down in worship before their roots, believing words to be pure only in their venerated origins; positivism, at the same time, nominalistically transmutes words into signs which it then processes arbitrarily, emptying language and revoking language's unifying power.

Of course, we cannot remain satisfied with this revelation of the true relationship between Heidegger's word-fetishism and the symbolic nominalism of the strict empirical sciences. In any event, organized scientific research has developed into a productive force in industrial society. The technical exploitation of its non-linguistic data sustains our lives – even if, at the level that Heinrich has in view, it also threatens the destruction of life insofar as the dialectical task of "translation" fails. Surely it is a question of restoring a pragmatically rich form of knowledge, not just in terms of the instrumental capacities of technically adept humanity, but also in terms of the linguistic possession of a communicative society – it is a matter of the re-translation of the products of the sciences back into the horizon of the lifeworld. But could we successfully undo the positivistically driven process of scientific research once the traces of the last of the ontologies have been swept away?

Translation, the wakening pronouncement, counts as the key to redemption. For Heinrich, life itself becomes synonymous with participation in language, reality synonymous with linguistic reality. This seems to me to be comprehensible from the perspective of Tillich's theology of personification, but as a consequence of the current of anti-ontological arguments inspired by Walter Benjamin, not entirely consistent. Had Heinrich seriously pursued the positivistic form of speechlessness (the operational use of signs in formalized languages) or the peculiar drive of formal logic toward explicitness (against which he offers the ambiguity of dialectical refusal), he would have discovered the system of social labor precisely in the "betrayal" that sustains the modern sciences. His theological approach, it seems, restricts his view to the origin of the process in whose course the human race wrests maturity from the "powers." Thus, mythical beginnings are not in the end referred to the categories of developed society, whose speechlessness is in fact the author's concern: he does not conceive language in its mediation through labor.

This may have something to do with the fact that, in the end, Heinrich believes that he can summarize his insights under the title of a new existentialism: instead of the anxiety of fundamental ontology, he proposes the "whirlpool" [*Sog*] – an odd regression into the very ontology that had fallen prey to his criticism.

Translated by Max Pensky

Note

1 Klaus Heinrich, *Versuch über die Schwierigkeit, Nein zu sagen* (Frankfurt am Main: Suhrkamp, 1964).

3

Transcendence from Within, Transcendence in this World

Allow me to make a personal remark to facilitate the start of a difficult discussion. I have continually responded to objections from my colleagues in philosophy and sociology.[1] Here, I again gladly respond to the criticism of Fred Dallmayr and Robert Wuthnow. Up until now, I have held back from a discussion with theologians; I would also prefer to continue to remain silent. A silence on the grounds of embarrassment would also be justified, for I am not really familiar with the theological discussion, and only reluctantly move about in an insufficiently reconnoitered terrain. On the other hand, for decades theologians both in Germany and in the United States have included me in their discussions. They have referred in general to the tradition of critical theory,[2] and have reacted to my writings.[3] In this situation, silence would be a false response: the person who is addressed and remains silent, clothes himself or herself in an aura of indeterminate significance and imposes silence. For this, Heidegger is one example among many. Because of this authoritarian character, Sartre has rightly called silence "reactionary."

I will start by first ascertaining a few premises under which theologians and philosophers today speak to one another, insofar as they share a self-critical assessment of modernity. Then, I will make an attempt to understand the status and truth claim of theological discourse. Following this, I will take up the most important objections from the theological side and, at the end, take a position on the criticism of the nontheologians in this volume.

Common Premises

From a distance, it is easier to speak about one another than with one another. For sociologists, it is easier to explain religious traditions and their roles from the perspective of an observer than to approach them in a performative stance. For sociologists, as long as they do not step out of their professional role, the change to the stance of an actual participant in religious discourse can only have the methodological sense of a hermeneutical intermediary step. A slightly different situation results for philosophers, at least for one who has grown up at German universities with Fichte, Schelling, and Hegel, including the latter's Marxist legacy. For, from this perspective, there is excluded from the start an approach that would merely objectify Jewish and Christian traditions, especially the speculatively fruitful Jewish and Protestant mysticism of the early modern period as mediated through the Swabian pietism of Bengel and Oetinger. Just as German Idealism with the concept of the Absolute appropriated theoretically the God of creation and of gracious love, it also with a logical reconstruction of the process of the world as a whole appropriated theoretically the traces of salvation history. Also, Kant cannot be understood without recognizing the motive of conceiving the essentially practical contents of the Christian tradition in such a way that these could perdure before the forum of reason. But contemporaries were fully aware of the ambiguity of these attempts at transformation. With the concept of "sublation" [*Aufhebung*] Hegel included this ambiguity in the dialectical method itself. The sublation of the world of religious representation in the philosophical concept enabled the saving of its essential contents only by casting off the substance of its piety. Certainly, the atheistic core, enveloped in esoteric insight, was reserved for the philosophers. Thus the later Hegel trusted philosophical reason only with the power of *partial* reconciliation. He had given up his hope in the concrete universality of that public religion which – according to the "Oldest System Program" – was to make the people rational and the philosophers sensible. The people are abandoned by their priests, now become philosophers.[4]

The *methodical* atheism of Hegelian philosophy and of all philosophical appropriation of essentially religious contents (which does not assert anything about the personal self-understanding of the philosophical author) became an open scandal only after Hegel's death as the "process of decay of the absolute spirit" (Marx) set in. The right-Hegelians, who to this day have reacted only defensively to this scandal, have yet to furnish a convincing response. For under the conditions of postmetaphysical thinking, it is not enough to take shelter behind a concept of the Absolute which can neither be freed from the concepts of the Hegelian "logic," nor be defended without a reconstruction of Hegelian dialectic that would be insightful *today* and would be joined to our philosophical discourses.[5] Clearly, the Young Hegelians did not recognize with equal acuity that along with fundamental metaphysical concepts, a metaphysically affirmed atheism is also no longer tenable. In whatever form materialism may appear, within the horizon of a scientific, fallibilistic mode of thinking it is a hypothesis which at best can claim plausibility for the present moment.

In our parts of the world, the grounds for a politically motivated atheism or, better, for a militant *laicism* have also, by and large, fallen away. During my time as a student, it was, above all, theologians such as Gollwitzer and Iwand who had given morally responsible answers to the political questions that challenged us after the war. It was the Confessing Church which at that time with its acknowledgment of guilt at least attempted a new beginning. In both confessions, leftist associations were formed, by lay people as well as theologians, who sought to free the church from its comfortable alliances with the power of the state and the existing social conditions. They sought renewal instead of restoration and to establish universal standards of judgment in the public political realm. With this exemplary witness and widely effective change of mentality there arose the model of a religious engagement which broke away from the conventionality and interiority of a merely private confession. With an undogmatic understanding of transcendence and faith, this engagement took seriously this-worldly goals of human dignity and social emancipation. It joined in a multivoiced arena with other forces pressing for radical democratization.

Against the background of a praxis which all would respect, we encounter a critical theology that interprets the self-understanding of this praxis in such a way that it helps express our best moral intuitions without tearing down the bridges to secular languages and cultures. Schüssler Fiorenza's fundamental theology offers a good example of a political theology that is in touch with contemporary investigations in morality and in social theory.[6] He first characterizes in a threefold manner the transformations that both religion and theology undergo under the conditions of postmetaphysical thinking, conditions that have become inescapable in modernity.[7] He emphasizes the uncoupling of a religion which is both interiorized and at the same time open to the secularized world from the explanatory claims of cosmological world views. The *Glaubenslehre* [*The Christian Faith*] in Schleiermacher's sense casts off the character of a cosmological world view. As a consequence of the recognition of the pluralism of religious forces, there ensues a reflective relationship to the particularity of one's own faith within the horizon of the universality of the religious as such. Joined with this is the insight that the ethical approaches which have emerged from the contexts of various world religions agree in the basic principles of a universalist morality. In a further step, Schüssler Fiorenza expounds the limits of a philosophical theory of morality which confines itself to the explanation and the grounding of the moral standpoint. He also discusses subsequent problems which arise from the abstractions of such an ethics of justice.

Since a philosophy which has become self-critical does not trust itself any longer to offer universal assertions about the concrete whole of exemplary forms of life, it must refer those affected to discourses in which they answer their substantial questions themselves. The parties should examine in moral argumentation what is equally good for all. But first they must become clear about what the good is for themselves in their respective contexts. These ethical questions in a stricter sense, concerning a life that is worthwhile [*nichtverfehlten*] or is preferable, can find an answer only in context-dependent discourses of self-understanding. These answers will be more differentiated and more appropriate depending upon how rich the identity-building traditions are that support self-reassurance [*Selbstvergewisserung*]. As Schüssler Fiorenza states using the words of Rawls, the question about one's own identity – who we are and desire to be – requires a "thick concept of the good." Thus each party must bring into the discussion his or her conceptions of the good and preferable life in order to find out with other parties what they all might desire. He suggests a "dialectic between universalizable principles of justice and the reconstructive hermeneutic of normative tradition" and attributes to the churches in modern society the role of being "communities of interpretation in which issues of justice and conceptions of goodness are publicly discussed" (86). Today the ecclesial communities are in competition with other communities of interpretation that are rooted in secular traditions. Even viewed from outside, it could turn out that monotheistic traditions have at their disposal a language whose semantic potential is not yet exhausted [*unabgegoltenen*], that shows itself to be superior in its power to disclose the world and to form identity, in its capability for renewal, its differentiation, and its range.

What I find interesting to observe in this example is that where theological argumentation is pushed so far into the neighborhood of other discourses, the perspectives from within and without meet without restraint. In this sense, I also understand those "correlational methods," which David Tracy employs for the "public theologies" widespread in the United States. These methods have the goal of placing in a relation of mutual critique interpretations of modernity proceeding from philosophical and social-theoretical approaches with theological interpretations of the Christian tradition. Thus, their goal is to bring these interpretations into a relation where arguments are used. This intention is facilitated when the projects of Enlightenment and of theology that Helmut Peukert discusses are described in similar ways from both sides: "The thesis seems plausible to me that the unsolved problem of advanced civilizations is that of mastering the tendency toward power accumulation."[8] Matthew Lamb observes how this tendency becomes critical in modernity and brings forth two false reactions, a romantic one and a historicist one. He pleads for a self-reassurance of modernity which breaks out of the cycle of a pernicious back and forth between nihilistic condemnation and dogmatic self-assertion: "Modern dogmatic self-assertion is profoundly nihilistic, just as modern nihilism is irresponsibly dogmatic."[9] Tracy specifies the concept of reason which guides a diagnosis of this kind. The dual failure of positivism and of the philosophy of consciousness confirms the pragmatic turn that took place from Peirce through Dewey toward a non-fundamentalist concept of communicative reason. At the same time, this concept opposes the conclusions that Rorty and Derrida draw from this failure, whether in the form of a radical contextualism or by way of an aesthetization of theory. Just as strongly, Tracy objects to selective modes of reading that leave out the ambivalent sense of modernization and perceive it merely as the history of the decay of a subject-centered reason that progresses forward in a linear manner and inflates itself up to be the totality. Even in modernity, reason has not withered into instrumental reason: "If understanding is dialogical, it is also . . . both historical and contextual. But . . . [a]ny act of understanding implicitly puts forward a claim to more than subjective understanding. Any act of understanding addresses all others with a claim to its validity – a validity that, in principle, the inquirer is obliged to redeem if challenged."[10]

Tracy draws from this pragmatic insight consequences also for the activity of theology itself which would be disciplined [*wissenschaftliche*] work and in no way simply a gift of faith. Peukert understands the work of theology as a methodically controlled form of religion. Gary Simpson compares the lifeworld, which reproduces itself through communicative action and validity claims that are open to critique, with a "forensically fraught world" and suggests that on the cross even God submits to this forum. Hence, none of the lifeworld's segments can immunize themselves against the demands for an argumentative justification, not even – as I understand the sentence – theology.[11] If this, however, is the *common ground* of theology, science, and philosophy, what then still constitutes the distinctiveness of theological discourse? What separates the internal perspective of theology from the external perspective of those who enter into a dialogue with theology? It cannot be the relation to religious discourses in general, but only the nature of the reference to the discourse conducted within each particular religious community.

The Truth Claim of Theological Discourse

Schüssler Fiorenza appeals to the line of tradition from Schleiermacher down to Bultmann and Niebuhr when he distinguishes a critical theology from neo-Aristotelian and neo-Thomist theologies. The great example of Karl Barth demonstrates, indeed, that the consistent unburdening of theology from metaphysical-cosmological explanatory claims does not mean *eo ipso* the willingness to assert that theological arguments have the power to convince in the debate with scientific discourses. From the Barthian viewpoint, the biblically witnessed event of revelation in its historical facticity rejects a mode of argumentation based on reason alone.[12] In the Protestant-shaped milieu of German universities, theological faculties have always enjoyed a special status. The young history of the University of Frankfurt dramatically shows this tension. When in the 1920s theological lectureships were to be introduced there, controversies broke out which could then only be settled by refusing to recognize the Catholic, Protestant, and Jewish subjects of study as specifically *theological* teaching. At this university, which grew out of a business college, it is interesting that in its social science atmosphere personalities such as Steinbüchel, Buber, and Tillich were able to establish themselves. It was thus political theologians in the broadest sense who could move about with ease in the discourses of the humanities and the social sciences.[13] In the Federal Republic of Germany, if I am right, it was primarily a group of Catholic theologians who, having always maintained a less troubled relation to the *lumen naturale*, were able to draw upon this tradition. Yet, the more that theology opens itself in general to the discourses of the human sciences, the greater is the danger that its own status will be lost in the network of alternating takeover attempts.

The *religious* discourse conducted within the communities of the faithful takes place in the context of a specific tradition with substantive norms and an elaborated dogmatics. It refers to a common ritual praxis and bases itself on the specifically religious experiences of the individual. It is, however, more than the non-objectifying, hermeneutically understanding reference to religious discourse and to the experiences underlying this discourse that characterizes theology. For the same would hold for a philosophy which understands itself as the critical appropriation and transformation, as the retrieval, of essential religious contents in the universe of argumentative discourse. This Hegelian self-understanding of philosophy has also not been abandoned by the materialistic students of Hegel. It lives on especially in Bloch, Benjamin, and in critical theory. True, Hegel was the last in an idealistic tradition that upheld the claim of metaphysics in a transformed shape, and completed the philosophical appropriation of the Judeo-Christian tradition as much as was possible under the conditions of metaphysical thinking. Hegel's philosophy is the result of that great experiment, crucially defining European intellectual history, which sought to produce a synthesis between the faith of Israel and the Greek spirit – a synthesis that, on the one side, led to the Hellenization of Christianity and, on the other, to the ambiguous Christianization of Greek metaphysics. The dialectical God of the philosophers allows the alter ego of prayer to fade away into anonymous thoughts of the Absolute. At least since Kierkegaard, this synthesis has become fragile, because it has been put into question from *both* sides.

In the same way as Adorno's philosophical critique, the theological protest of Johann Baptist Metz is directed against the fundamental concepts of a metaphysics which, even when they have been dialectically set in motion, remain too rigid to be able to retrieve rationally those experiences of redemption, universal alliance, and irreplaceable individuality which have been articulated in the language of the Judeo-Christian history of salvation without truncating them and reducing the fullness of their specific meanings. Metz insists with Benjamin upon the anamnestic constitution of reason and wants to understand the faith of Israel also from its own historical spirit.[14] Adorno circumscribes the non-identical and seeks to think with the aid of concepts beyond all objectifying concepts, because he follows the same impulse: to save intuitions that have not been exhausted in philosophy. Here it is the experience of an equality that does not level out difference and of a togetherness that individualizes. It is the experience of a closeness across distance to an other acknowledged in his or her difference. It is the experience of a combination of autonomy and self-surrender, a reconciliation which does not extinguish the differences, a future-oriented justice that is in solidarity with the unreconciled suffering of past generations. It is the experience of the reciprocity of freely granted acknowledgment, of a relationship in which a subject is associated to another without being submitted to the degrading violence of exchange – a derisive violence that allows for the happiness and power of the one only at the price of the unhappiness and powerlessness of the other.

If, however, this *anti-Platonic turn* takes place on both sides, then it cannot be the postmetaphysical kind of reference to religious discourse that today separates philosophy from a theology open to conversation. Rather, under the conditions of postmetaphysical thought another difference, which was surrounded by ambiguities up until Hegel, clearly emerges: methodical atheism in the manner of the philosophical reference to the contents of religious experience. Philosophy cannot appropriate what is talked about in religious discourse *as* religious experiences. These experiences could only be added to the fund of philosophy's resources, recognized as philosophy's own basis of experience, if philosophy identifies these experiences using a description that is no longer borrowed from the language of a specific religious tradition, but from the universe of argumentative discourse that is uncoupled from the event of revelation. At those fracture points where a neutralizing translation of this type can no longer succeed, philosophical discourse must confess its failure. The metaphorical use of words such as "redemption," "messianic light," "restoration of nature," etc., makes religious experience a mere citation. In these moments of its powerlessness, argumentative speech passes over beyond religion and science into literature, into a mode of presentation that is no longer directly measured by truth claims. In an analogical way, theology also loses its identity if it only cites religious experiences, and under the descriptions of religious discourse no longer acknowledges them as its own basis. Therefore, I hold that a conversation cannot succeed between a theology and a philosophy which use the language of religious authorship and which meet on the bridge of religious experiences that have become literary expressions.

Admittedly, theology which wants to subject itself without reservation to scientific argumentation, as Tracy and Peukert emphasize, will not be satisfied with the limiting criterion that I have proposed. What does "methodical atheism" really mean? To answer this question, I would like to digress a moment.

Religious discourse is closely joined to a ritual praxis that, in comparison with profane everyday praxis, is limited in the degree of its freedom of communication in a specific way. If a functionalist description is permitted, then it could be said that faith is protected against a radical problematization by its being rooted in cult. This problematization unavoidably occurs when the ontic, normative, and expressive aspects of validity, which must remain fused together in the conception of the creator and redeemer God, of theodicy, and of the event of salvation, are separated analytically from one another.[15] Theological discourse, however, distinguishes itself from religious by separating itself from ritual praxis in the act of explaining it, for example that it *interprets* sacraments such as baptism or the eucharist. Theology for its assertions also aspires to a truth claim that is differentiated from the spectrum of the other validity claims. Yet, beyond the measure of uncertainty that all reflection brings as it intrudes upon practical knowledge, theology did not present a danger to the faith of the community as long as it used the basic concepts of metaphysics. Indeed, these metaphysical concepts were immune to a differentiation of the aspects of validity in a fashion similar to the basic religious concepts. This situation only changed with the collapse of metaphysics. Under the conditions of postmetaphysical thinking, whoever puts forth a truth claim today must, nevertheless, translate experiences that have their home in religious discourse into the language of a scientific expert culture – and from this language retranslate them back into praxis.

This task of translation demanded by critical theology can be formally compared with that which modern philosophy also has to undertake. For philosophy stands in a similarly intimate relationship to common sense which it reconstructs and at the same time undermines. In the opposite direction, philosophy functions in the role of an interpreter that should carry essential contents of the expert culture back into everyday praxis. This task of mediation is not free of a certain paradox, because in the expert cultures knowledge is treated under respectively separate aspects of validity, whereas in everyday praxis *all* linguistic functions and aspects of validity are interwoven and form a syndrome.[16] Nevertheless, philosophy, in a way, has an easier task dealing with common sense, from which it lives and which it at the same time reforms, than does theology with the religious discourses given to it. Today, between these discourses and profane everyday praxis, there is certainly no longer the same distance that once existed between the sacred and the profane spheres of life – and this distance even continues to decrease as the ideas of a "public theology" gain acceptance. But against the reform to which common sense is subject in modern societies, whether with the assistance of philosophers or not, that syndrome of revelation faith, held together in ritualized praxis, still forms a specific barrier. For religious discourses would lose their identity if they were to open themselves up to a type of interpretation which no longer allows the religious experiences to be valid *as* religious.

One must expect, after all, such a far-reaching problematization if theological discourse no longer chooses either of the two premises that are characteristic of modern theology. After Kierkegaard, theology has either taken the "Protestant path" and appealed to the kerygma and faith as a source of religious insight absolutely independent of reason, or has chosen the path of "enlightened Catholicism" in the sense that it relinquishes the status of a special discourse and exposes its assertions to the whole range of scientific discussion. Admittedly, it does this without renouncing the acknowledgment of the experiences articulated in the language of the Judeo-Christian tradition as its *own* base of experience. It is this reservation alone which permits a distanciation from the language game of religious discourses without invalidating it. It leaves the religious language game intact. The third way, however, is characterized by what I have called "methodical atheism." It is this way that leads to a program of demythologization that is tantamount to an experiment. Without reservation it is left to the realization of this program to see whether the theological (not just a history of religions) interpretation of the religious discourses by virtue of its argumentation alone permits a joining to the scientific discussion in such a manner that the religious language game remains intact, or collapses. I see the "political dogmatics" of the Copenhagen theologian Jens Glebe-Möller as an example of such an experiment.

Building upon the theoretical approaches of Apel, Döbert, and myself and supported by a discourse ethics, Glebe-Möller subjects the Christian dogmas to a demythologizing interpretation, which recalls for me a saying of Hugo Ball: God is the freedom of the lowliest in the spiritual communication of all. Glebe-Möller interprets baptism, the eucharist, the imitation of Christ, the role of the church, and eschatology in the sense of a theology of liberation based on a theory of communication, which opens up the Bible in a fascinating (for me, also convincing) way, even in those passages that have become foreign to modern ears. But I ask myself *who* recognizes himself or herself in this interpretation.

Does the Christian language game remain intact if one understands the idea of God in the way that Glebe-Möller proposes it? "The thought of a personified divine power necessarily involves heteronomy, and this is an idea that goes directly against the modern concept of human autonomy. A political dogmatic in the modern context must therefore be atheistic. But this does not mean that there is no thinking about God or that the thought of God is emptied of all content."[17] Taking up a reflection of Peukert's, he explains this as follows:

> If we desire to hold on to solidarity with everyone else in the communicative fellowship, even the dead . . . then we must claim a reality that can reach beyond the here and how, or that can connect our selves beyond our own death with those who went innocently to their destruction before us. And it is this reality that the Christian tradition calls God. (110)

But in contrast to Peukert, Glebe-Möller insists on an *atheistic version* of this idea in that he poses the question:

> But are we not then back at the point where only faith in a divine deliverance can rescue us – where, with Peukert, we have to reintroduce the thought of God? I continue to be convinced that we are today unable to think that thought. This means that the guilt remains in effect. Instead of resigning ourselves to it, however, we must make the consciousness of guilt into something positive, something that spurs us to fight against the conditions that have produced the guilt. That can happen when we hold fast to our solidarity with all who have suffered and died, now and before. This solidarity or fellowship contains within itself a "messianic" power that transforms any passive consciousness of guilt into an active struggle against the conditions for guilt – just as it was when Jesus, who, two thousand years ago, forgave sinners and set people free to continue that struggle.
>
> But *can* we be in solidarity? In the last analysis, we can be nothing else, for solidarity – the ideal communicative fellowship – is presupposed in everything we say and do! (112)

Theological Objections

The theologians who in this volume have entered into a dialogue with me would hardly want to be bound to one of the three alternatives that I have named. They want to follow the path of radical demythologizations as little as they want to follow the classical Protestant path which in our century led to Karl Barth. Yet these same theologians may not consider valid for themselves the reservation that I associated with the characterization and the name of "enlightened Catholicism." For settling on a basis of experience which remains bound a priori to the language of a specific tradition signifies a particularistic limitation of the truth claims of theology. Yet, as truth claims they extend beyond all merely local contexts – and for David Tracy this is not open to negotiation. Consistent with this, my theological dialogue partners therefore choose the indirect procedure of apologetic argumentation and attempt to force the secular opponent into a corner by way of an immanent critique such that the opponent can find a way out of the aporias demonstrated only by conceding the theologically defended affirmations.

Helmut Peukert masterfully employs this technique in his major investigation, *Science, Action, and Fundamental Theology*.[18] He first of all criticizes, as does David Tracy, the one-sided, functionalist description that I gave of religion in *The Theory of Communicative Action*. Even in traditional societies, the world religions do *not* function *exclusively* as a legitimation of governmental authority: "in their origin and in their core, they are often protest movements against the basic trend of a society's development and attempt to ground other ways for human beings to relate to one another and to reality as a whole."[19] I will not dispute this. I would also admit that I subsumed rather too hastily the development of religion in modernity with Max Weber under the "privatization of the powers of faith" and suggested too quickly an affirmative answer to the question as to "whether then from religious truths, after the religious world views have collapsed, nothing more and nothing other than the secular principles of a universalist ethics of responsibility can be salvaged, and this means: can be accepted for good reasons, on the basis of insight."[20] This question has to *remain open* from the view of the social scientist who proceeds reconstructively and who is careful not simply to project developing trends forward in a straight line. It must also remain open from the viewpoint of the philosopher who appropriates tradition and who in a performative stance has the experience that intuitions which had long been articulated in religious language can neither be rejected nor simply retrieved rationally – as I have shown with the example of the concept of individuality.[21] The process of a critical appropriation of the essential contents of religious tradition is still underway and the outcome is difficult to predict. I willingly repeat my position: "As long as religious language bears with itself inspiring, indeed, unrelinquishable semantic contents which elude (for the moment?) the expressive power of a philosophical language and still await translation into a discourse that gives reasons for its positions, philosophy, even in its postmetaphysical form, will neither be able to replace nor to repress religion."[22]

This still does not imply any agreement with Peukert's thesis that the discourse theory of morality and ethics gets so entangled in limit questions that it finds itself in need of a theological foundation. Of course, effective socializing or pedagogical praxis, which under the aegis of an anticipated autonomy [*Mündigkeit*] seeks to provoke freedom in the other, must take into account the appearance of circumstances and spontaneous forces that it cannot at the same time control. And, with an orientation toward unconditional moral expectations, the subject increases the degree of his or her vulnerability. This then makes the subject especially dependent upon a considerate moral treatment from other persons. Yet, the risk of failure, indeed, of the annihilation of freedom precisely in the processes that should promote and realize freedom, only attests to the constitution of our finite existence. I refer to the necessity, which Peirce emphasized again and again, of a self-relinquishing, transcending anticipation of an unlimited community of communication. This anticipation is simultaneously conceded to us and demanded of us. In communicative action, we orient ourselves toward validity claims that, practically, we can raise only in the context of *our* languages and of our forms of life, even if the convertibility [*Einlösbarkeit*] that we implicitly co-posit *points beyond* the provinciality of our respective historical standpoints. We are exposed to the movement of a transcendence from within, which is just as little at our disposal as the actuality of the spoken word turns us into masters of the structure of language (or of the Logos). The anamnestically constituted reason, which Metz and Peukert, rightly, continually advocate in opposition to a Platonically reduced communicative reason that is insensitive to the temporal dimension, confronts us with the conscientious question about deliverance for the annihilated victims. In this way we become aware of the limits of that transcendence from within which is directed to this world. But this does not enable us to ascertain the *countermovement* of a compensating transcendence from beyond.

That the universal covenant of fellowship would be able to be effective retroactively, toward the past, only in the weak medium of our memory, of the remembrance of the living generations, and of the anamnestic witnesses handed down falls short of our moral need. But the painful experience of a deficit is still not a sufficient argument for the assumption of an "absolute freedom which saves in death."[23] The postulate of a God "which is outlined in temporal, finite, self-transcending intersubjective action in the form of a hopeful expectation [*Erwartung*]"[24] relies upon an experience that is either recognized as such in the language of religious discourse – or loses its evidence. Peukert himself resorts to an experience *accessible only in the language of the Christian tradition*, interwoven inseparably with religious discourse: that with the death on the cross, the disastrous web of evil has been broken. Without this "anticipatory" [*zuvorkommende*] goodness of God, a solidarity among human beings who

acknowledge one another unconditionally remains without the guarantee of an outcome that extends beyond the individual act and the
moment of illumination this ignites in the eye of the other. It is,
indeed, true that whatever human beings succeed in doing they owe
to those rare constellations in which their own powers are able to be
joined with the favorableness of the historical moment. But the experience that we are dependent upon this favorableness is still no
license for the assumption of a divine promise of salvation.

Charles Davis takes up the same apologetic figure of thought when
he wants to show that the moral viewpoint implied in the structure
of a praxis directed toward reaching agreement, as well as the
perspective of living together in solidarity and justice, remain
ungrounded without a foundation in Christian hope: "A secular
hope without religion cannot affirm with certainty . . . a future
fulfillment."[25] Once again I do not see why a *superadditum* is
indispensable in order that we would endeavor to act according to
moral commands and ethical insights as long as these require something that is objectively possible. It is true that a philosophy that
thinks postmetaphysically cannot answer the question that Tracy also
calls attention to: why be moral at all? At the same time, however,
this philosophy can show why this question does not arise meaning-
fully for communicatively socialized individuals. We acquire our
moral intuitions in our parents' home, not in school. And moral
insights tell us that we do not have any good reasons for behaving
otherwise: for this, no self-surpassing of morality is necessary. It is
true that we often behave otherwise, but we do so with a bad conscience. The first half of the sentence attests to the weakness of
the motivational power of good reasons; the second half attests that
rational motivation by reasons is more than nothing [*auch nicht
nichts ist*] – moral convictions do not allow themselves to be over-
ridden without resistance.

All of this does yet not treat that struggle against the conditions
that have caused us to fail again and again. Glebe-Möller, Davis,
Peukert, and others have in view not only the observance of concrete
obligations. They seek also a far-reaching engagement for the aboli-
tion of unjust conditions and the promotion of forms of life that
would not only make solidary action more likely but first make it
possible for this action to be reasonably expected. Who or what gives
us the courage for such a total engagement that in situations of depri-
vation and degradation is already being expressed when the destitute

and deprived summon the energy each morning to carry on anew? The question about the meaning of life is not meaningless. Nevertheless, the circumstance that penultimate arguments inspire no great confidence is not enough for the grounding of a hope that can be kept alive only in a religious language. The thoughts and expectations directed toward the common good have, after metaphysics has collapsed, only an unstable status. In the place of an Aristotelian politics and a Hegelian philosophy of history, a post-Marxist social theory that has become more humble has appeared. This social theory attempts to exhaust the potential for argumentation in the human sciences in order to contribute to assertions about the genesis, constitution, and ambivalent development of modernity. These diagnoses, even if they are somewhat reliably grounded, remain controversial. Above all they perform a critical service. They can take apart the mutual prejudices of affirmative theories of progress and of negativist theories of decline, of patchwork ideologies and premature totalizations. But, in the passage through the discursive universes of science and philosophy, not even the Peircean hope in a fallible theory of the development of being as a whole, including that of the *summum bonum*, will be able to be realized. Kant already had answered the question "What may we hope for?" with a *postulate* of practical reason, not with a premodern certainty that could inspire us with *confidence*.

I believe to have shown that in communicative action we have no choice but to presuppose the idea of an undistorted intersubjectivity. This, again, can be understood as the formal characterization of the necessary conditions for the forms, not able to be anticipated, of a worthwhile life. There is no theory for these totalities themselves. Certainly, praxis requires encouragement; it is inspired by intuitive anticipations of the whole. There is an intuition that impresses me deeply which I have occasionally formulated: If historical progress consists in lessening, abolishing, or preventing the suffering of vulnerable creatures, and if historical experience teaches that on the heels of advances finally achieved, consuming disaster closely follows, then there are grounds for supposing that the balance of what can be endured remains intact only if we give our utmost for the sake of the possible advances.[26] Perhaps it is such assumptions which, indeed, can give no confidence for a praxis whose certainties have been taken away, yet can still leave it some hope.

To reject apologetic figures of thought is one thing; it is another thing to learn from the worthy objections of my theological colleagues. I leave aside here the reservations that David Tracy brings forth against approaches based on an evolutionary theory and shall concentrate on his thesis that dialogue, and not argumentation, offers the more encompassing approach for the investigation of communicative action.

Augumentative discourse is certainly the more specialized form of communication. In it validity claims which previously remained implicit because they arose performatively are expressly thematized. Therefore, they have a reflexive character that requires the more exacting presuppositions of communication. The presuppositions of action oriented toward reaching understanding are more easily accessible in argumentation. This preference as part of a research strategy does not imply an ontological distinction, as if argumentation would be more important or even more fundamental than conversation or the communicative everyday praxis constituted in the lifeworld. This everyday praxis forms the most encompassing horizon. In this sense, even the analysis of speech acts enjoys only a heuristic preference. This analysis of speech acts forms the key for a pragmatic analysis which, as Tracy rightly insists, must comprise the entire spectrum of the world of symbolic forms: symbols and images, indicators and expressive gestures, as well as relations of similarity. Thus, it must extend to all signs that lie beneath the level of propositionally differentiated speech, signs that can represent semantic contents even if they have no author who bestows meaning upon them. The semiotics of Charles S. Peirce has made accessible this archaeology of signs. The richness of this theory is far from being exhausted; this is also true for an aesthetics that points out the world-disclosing function of works of art in their speechless materiality.

Tracy repeats the criticism concerning the reductions of an expressivistic aesthetics which *The Theory of Communicative Action* at least suggested. In the meantime, in response to the works of Albrecht Wellmer and Martin Seel,[27] I have corrected this.[28] Although an innovative world-disclosing power belongs to both prophetic speech as well as to art that has become autonomous, I would hesitate to name religious and aesthetic symbols in the same breath. I am certain that David Tracy in no way wants to suggest an aesthetic understanding of the religious. Aesthetic experience has become an integral component of the modern world in that it has become independent as a cultural sphere of value. Religion would be stabilized by a similar differentiation into a social subsystem specialized, as Niklas Luhmann holds, in coping with contingency, but only at the price of the complete neutralization of its experiential content. In opposition to this, political theology also fights for a public role for religion and precisely in modern societies. Yet then religious symbolism should not conform to the aesthetic, that is, to the forms of expression of an expert culture, but must maintain its *holistic* position in the lifeworld.

Furthermore, I take very seriously Peukert's warning to take into account the temporal dimensions of action that is oriented toward reaching understanding. Nevertheless, phenomenological analyses in the style of *Being and Time* cannot simply be transplanted into a theory of communication. Possibly, Peirce's semiotics offers a better and, until now, unused entry point. Karl-Otto Apel and I have, up to now, appropriated only the fundamental insight of his theory of truth, that a transcending power dwells within validity claims which assures a relation to the future for every speech act: "Thus thought is rational only so far as it recommends itself to a possible future thought. Or in other words the rationality of thought lies in its reference to a possible future."[29] But the young Peirce had already given an interesting reference to the ability of the sign process to establish continuity. In epistemological contexts, he ascribes to the individual symbol the power to produce that continuity in the flow of our experiences that Kant wanted to ascertain through the accompanying "I-think" of transcendental apperception. Because the individual experience itself assumes the threefold structure of a sign that refers simultaneously to a past object and to a future interpretant, this experience can come into a semantic relation to other experiences across temporal distances and thus establish a temporal connection upon a diversity which otherwise, as in a kaleidoscope, would fall apart.[30] In this way, Peirce explains temporal relations that are only first produced through the structure of signs. The medium of language could borrow from this semiotic structure its dynamic of temporalization that is unfolded in the continuities of tradition.

Finally, I respond to the objections that are not motivated by specifically theological considerations.

Response to the Nontheologians

1. Sheila Briggs makes distinctions within the paradigm of praxis philosophy that I find plausible. However, I still do not quite see how under her premises one can reach the type of dialogical ethics that will ground the universal accountability and the integrity of the particular identity of each person without claiming the universalist viewpoints of equality and justice. Seyla Benhabib, on whose works Briggs supports her feminist critique, also remains faithful to the universalist intentions of Kant and Hegel. Benhabib develops her conception thoroughly in agreement with me:

> While agreeing that normative disputes can be rationally settled, and that fairness, reciprocity, and some procedure of universalizability are constituents, that is necessary conditions of the moral standpoint, interactive universalism regards difference as a starting point for reflection and action. In this sense "universality" is a regulative ideal that does not deny our embodied and embedded identity, but aims at developing moral attitudes and encouraging political transformations that can yield a view acceptable to all. Universality is not the ideal consensus of fictitiously defined selves, but the concrete process in politics and morals of the struggle of concrete, embodied selves, striving for autonomy.[31]

Nevertheless, Benhabib questions the limitation of moral argumentation to problems of justice, because she believes that the logical distinction between questions of justice and questions about the good life is based on or, at least, corresponds to the sociological distinction between the public and private spheres. A morality curtailed legalistically, so she thinks, would have to restrict itself to questions of political justice. All private relations and personal spheres of life, which a patriarchal society leaves principally to women, are then excluded *per definitionem* from the sphere of responsibility of morality. This assumption, however, is not correct. For the logical distinction between problems of justice and of the good life is independent from the sociological distinction between spheres of life. We make a *moral* use of practical reason when we ask what is equally good for everyone; we make an *ethical* use when we ask what is respectively good for me or for us. Questions of justice permit under the moral viewpoint what all could will: answers that in principle are universally valid. Ethical questions, on the other hand, can be rationally clarified only in the context of a specific life-history or a particular form of life. For these questions are perspectively focused on the individual or on a specific collective who want to know who they are and, at the same time, who they want to be. Such processes of self-understanding distinguish themselves from moral argumentation in the way they pose the question, not however, in the gender-specific location of their themes.

That certainly does not mean that in moral questions we have to abstract from the concrete other. Briggs and Benhabib distinguish between two perspectives according to whether we respectively consider all those concerned in their entirety, or the particular individual in his or her situation. In moral argumentation, both perspectives must come into play. But they have to be intertwined. In *justification discourses* [*Begründungsdiskursen*], practical reason becomes effective through a principle of universalization, while individual cases are considered only as illustrative examples. Justified norms, admittedly, can claim only prima facie validity. Which norm in the individual case is held to be the most appropriate and, to that extent, has precedence over other, likewise prima facie valid norms cannot be decided in the same way. This application of norms requires instead a discourse of another type. Such *application discourses* [*Anwendungsdiskurse*] follow a logic different than that for justification discourses. Here, in fact, it is a question of the concrete other in the context of the respective given circumstances, the particular social relationships, the unique identity and life-history. Which norm is respectively the *appropriate* one can only be judged in the light of a description of all the relevant features that is as complete as possible.[32] If there is anything to hold against Lawrence Kohlberg, against whom Benhabib advances considerations from Carol Gilligan, then it is not his explanation of the moral principle on the basis of the process of the ideal role-taking, an explanation based upon George Herbert Mead, but his neglect of the problem of application.

2. At this point I can react only with a few remarks to the very thoughtful, but rather allusively presented criticism of Robert Wuthnow. A great deal of hermeneutical preparatory work would probably be necessary on both sides. Wuthnow is uneasy about the whole undertaking of a critical theory of society that reflexively retrieves, in a way, its context of origin, and which relies upon a rational potential found in the linguistic medium of socialization

itself.[33] He does not keep separate the different analytical levels and does not bear in mind the methodical difference between a formal-pragmatically performed theory of language, of argumentation, and of action, on the one hand, and a sociological theory of action and of systems, on the other hand. He does not distinguish between the concept of the lifeworld employed formal-pragmatically or sociologically. He also does not distinguish between a discourse theory of truth, of morality, and of justice which proceeds normatively, on the one hand, empirically substantive attempts at reconstruction that have a descriptive claim, on the other hand. This theoretical framework is certainly not unproblematic. But I don't see how his ad hoc objections can be properly discussed if there is not a closer understanding of the architectural plan.

For example, it is not the case that I oppose a radiant future to a devalued past. The proceduralist concept of rationality that I propose cannot sustain utopian projects for concrete forms of life as a whole. The theory of society within which my analyses take place can at best lead to diagnostic descriptions which allow the ambivalence of contrary tendencies of development to emerge more clearly. It is not a case of idealizing the future; if anything, in *The Structural Transformation of the Public Sphere*, there was on my part an idealization of the past.

It is correct that I advocate a pragmatic theory of meaning according to which a hearer understands an expression when he or she knows the conditions under which it can be accepted as valid. The basic idea is simple: one understands an expression only if one knows how one could utilize it in order to come to an understanding with anyone about something in the world. This internal relation between the process of reaching agreement and rationality is inferred from the methodically assumed attitude of a virtual participant. But from here there is no direct path that leads to a social-scientific rationalism which remains deaf to "personal freedom, willful violations of established norms, pluralism, and nonreductive modes of expressivity."[34] Wuthnow can recognize in communicative rationality, which is inherent in the medium of language, only an extension of instrumental rationality. In doing this, he is relying upon the analyses that were put forth at the beginning of the first volume of *The Theory of Communicative Action*, namely, that of the use of propositional knowledge in affirmations, on the one hand, and purposive-rational actions, on the other hand. He does not take into consideration that these two model cases form merely the starting point for a progressively expanded analysis. By the way, I consider information [*Mitteilung*] and norm-regulated action (as also expressive self-presentation) only as limit cases of communicative action. The contrast between an innovative and idiosyncratic use of language serves only the explanation of the use of evaluative expressions.

All these things must first be set right before Wuthnow's interesting remark concerning a resacralization of the lifeworld could be discussed. That is probably the real point of dispute: whether the liberation of everyday praxis from alienation and colonialization is to be described more in the sense that I hold, as a rationalization of the lifeworld, or in the sense of Odo Marquard as a "re-enchantment."[35]

3. Fred Dallmayr's paper on "Critical Theory and Reconciliation" presents me with some difficulties. With great understanding Dallmayr traces important religious background motifs in Horkheimer and Adorno's *Dialectic of Enlightenment* as well as in Adorno's later philosophy. He analyses in a manner similar to my own the aporias in which critical theory gets entangled. Against this background, he then subjects *The Theory of Communicative Action* to an astonishingly prejudiced critique. It is astonishing for the reason that Dallmayr is thoroughly acquainted with my writings. For decades, he has commented upon my publications not uncritically, but rather with great sensitivity and a comprehensive knowledge of the German discussion and its context.[36]

Dallmayr has set the course for the present dispute in an interesting essay on the question: "Is Critical Theory a Humanism?" In it the expression "humanism" is used pejoratively as with Heidegger and means as much as anthropocentrism. Dallmayr thinks that I merely exchange the transcendental subject for a quasi-transcendental intersubjectivity. To him, the linguistic turn of critical theory only veils the fact that beyond language subjectivity is reinstated in its Cartesian rights:

> Habermas's outlook . . . can with some legitimacy be described as a "humanism" – where this term stands for a more or less man- or subject-focused orientation. The distinctions between empiricism and hermeneutics, system and lifeworld and propositional and reflexive speech can, without undue violence, be reconciled with the Cartesian and Kantian subject-object bifurcation (and thus with the basic framework of metaphysics).[37]

This focus, naturally, must surprise an author who, in his own understanding, has pursued the pragmatic-linguistic turn as the critique of any form of a philosophy of the subject – certainly with enough caution as not to fall from the frying pan of subject-centered reason into the fire of a history of Being circumscribed by a negative metaphysics. Precisely this anti-Heideggerian accent to the paradigm shift might provoke Dallmayr into disavowing the paradigm shift itself.

This is especially difficult for me to understand in view of a book like *The Philosophical Discourse of Modernity*, in which I develop the new paradigm of the process of understanding from its context in the history of philosophy. My intention is to show how one can avoid the traps of the philosophy of the subject without entangling oneself at the same time in the aporias of a self-referential and totalizing critique of reason – neither in the deconstructionist version of the late Heideggerians nor in the contextualistic version of the late Wittgensteinians.[38] Since the argumentative substance of the third, critical part of Dallmayr's contribution is not sufficient for an extensive debate, I limit myself to a few cursory remarks.

a. Dallmayr supports his assertion of a "continuity" between the paradigm of the process of understanding and that of the subject-object relation with the point that speech acts demonstrate the same teleological structure as do purposive activities.[39] Yet, as I have argued elsewhere, the teleological language game has a different meaning in the theory of language than in the theory of action.[40] The same fundamental concepts are respectively interpreted in each case in a different sense – and, indeed, interpreted differently in a sense that is relevant for our question. In contrast to teleological actions, speech acts are directed toward illocutionary goals, which do not have the status of a purpose that is to be realized *innerworldly*. These goals also cannot be realized without the *uncoerced* cooperation and agreement of the one addressed and, finally, can be explained only through recourse to the concept of reaching agreement that is *inherent* in the medium of language itself. As opposed to teleological actions, speech acts in addition interpret themselves on the basis of their twofold illocutionary-propositional structure itself: by performing speech acts, one states at the same time what one does.

b. Dallmayr believes further that the theory of speech acts privileges the role of the speaker and does not take into account the accomplishments of the hearer (143). The opposite is the case for an analysis which insists (against Searle) that every action of speech remains incomplete without the "Yes" or "No" response of a potential hearer. The hearer must take the position of a second person, give up the perspective of an observer in favor of that of a participant, and enter into a lifeworld that is intersubjectively shared by a linguistic community if he or she wants to take advantage of the characteristic reflexivity of natural language. This thoroughly hermeneutical conception of language is directed against the theoreticism of the causalistic model of linguistic understanding shared by Quine, Davidson, and others.

c. Dallmayr then emphasizes the complementarity of speaking and silence: "language . . . reverberates with its own silence" (143). This reference to the ontological "unfathomability" of language clearly remains in needs of further elaboration beyond the mystical language allusions of the later Heidegger. If Dallmayr does not want to withdraw from the start the phenomenon of silence from an analysis of language, he can make use of my theory of communication: nonauratic silence draws from the specific context a more or less unmistakable meaning. Moreover, every speech act is, of course, situated, and every speech situation is embedded in an intersubjectively shared lifeworld context, which silently wreathes what is spoken in a mute presence.[41]

d. Furthermore, Dallmayr accuses me of having an instrumentalist conception of language (142ff.). This linguistic empiricism has already been overcome by Hamann and Humboldt. I, too, do not develop my theory of communication from Locke, but from hermeneutics and from American pragmatism. Clearly, the act of naming, which from the Romantic philosophy of language up to Benjamin has played a paradigmatic role (a role rich in associations with respect to Christian speculations about the Logos), has proved to be a rather one-sided model for the explanation of linguistically creative powers. In a strict interpretation, it leads to a conception of language based upon a semantics of reference. According to it, expressions should represent states of affairs in the same way that a name stands for an object – which is false. Just as incorrect is the speculative interpretation of the model of naming, which hypostatizes the constitutive, i.e., world-disclosing power of language and thereby neglects the relevance of the validity of language-enabled practices in the world (the confrontation with whatever is encountered in the world).

e. Finally, Dallmayr blames me for the restoration of a "shallow" (as it was called in Germany until 1945) Enlightenment Rationalism (132ff.). The shallow and the profound have their own pitfalls. I have always attempted to steer between the Scylla of a leveling, transcendence-less empiricism and the Charybdis of a high-flying idealism that glorifies transcendence. I hope to have learned much from Kant, and still I have not become a Dallmayrian Kantian because the theory of communicative action *integrates* the transcendental tension between the intelligible and the world of appearances in communicative everyday praxis, yet does not thereby *level* it out. The Logos of language founds the intersubjectivity of the lifeworld, in which we find ourselves already preunderstood, in order that we can encounter one another face to face as subjects. Indeed, we meet as subjects who impute to each other accountability, that is, the capability to guide our actions according to transcending validity claims. At the same time, the lifeworld reproduces itself through the medium of our communicative actions which are to be accounted for by us. Yet, this does not mean that the lifeworld would be at our disposal. As agents of communicative action, we are exposed to a transcendence that is integrated in the linguistic conditions of reproduction without being *delivered up* to it. This conception can hardly be identified with the productivist illusion of a species that generates itself and which puts itself in the place of a disavowed Absolute. Linguistic intersubjectivity goes beyond the subjects without putting them *in bondage* [*hörig*]. It is not a higher-level subjectivity and therefore, without sacrificing a transcendence from within, it can do without the concept of an Absolute. We can dispense with this legacy of Hellenized Christianity as well as with any subsequent right-Hegelian constructions, upon which Dallmayr still seems to rely.

Translated by Eric Crump and Peter P. Kenny

Notes

1 See my "A Postscript to *Knowledge and Human Interests*," in *Philosophy of the Social Sciences* 3 (1975): 157–89, as well as my replies in John B. Thompson and David Held, eds., *Habermas: Critical Debates* (Cambridge, Mass.: MIT Press, 1982); Richard J. Bernstein, ed., *Habermas and Modernity* (Cambridge, Mass.: MIT Press, 1985); and Axel Honneth and Hans Joas, eds., *Kommunikatives Handeln*

(Frankfurt am Main: Suhrkamp, 1986) [Axel Honneth and Hans Joas, eds., *Communicative Action* (Cambridge, Mass.: MIT Press, 1990)].

2   Hans-Georg Geyer, Hans-Norbert Janowski, and Alfred Schmidt, *Theologie und Soziologie* (Stuttgart: Kohlhammer, 1970); Rudolf J. Siebert, *The Critical Theory of Religion: The Frankfurt School* (Berlin/ New York/Amsterdam: Mouton, 1985).

3   See the impressive bibliography compiled by Edmund Arens in *Habermas und die Theologie. Beiträge zur theologischen Rezeption, Diskussion und Kritik der Theorie kommunikativen Handelns*, ed. Edmund Arens (Düsseldorf: Patmos, 1989), 9–38.

4   Jürgen Habermas, *The Philosophical Discourse of Modernity*, trans. Frederick Lawrence (Cambridge, Mass.: MIT Press, 1987), 35–41; see also Karl Löwith, "Hegels Aufhebung der christlichen Religion," in Karl Löwith, *Vorträge und Abhandlungen. Zur Kritik der christlichen Überlieferung* (Stuttgart: Kohlhammer, 1966), 54–96.

5   This appears to me to be the awkward situation in which Fred Dallmayr finds himself.

6   Francis Schüssler Fiorenza, *Foundational Theology: Jesus and the Church* (New York: Crossroad, 1984).

7   Francis Schüssler Fiorenza, "The Church as a Community of Interpretation: Political Theology between Discourse Ethics and Hermeneutical Reconstruction," in Don S. Browning and Francis Schüssler Fiorenza, eds., *Habermas, Modernity, and Public Theology* (New York, Crossroads, 1992). The page numbers in the text refer to this essay.

8   Helmut Peukert, "Enlightenment and Theology as Unfinished Projects," in Browning and Schüssler Fiorenza, eds., *Habermas, Modernity, and Public Theology*, 44.

9   Matthew Lamb, "Communicative Praxis and Theology: Beyond Modern Nihilism and Dogmatism," in Browning and Schüssler Fiorenza, eds., *Habermas, Modernity, and Public Theology*, 95.

10 David Tracy, "Theology, Critical Social Theory, and the Public Realm," in Browning and Schüssler Fiorenza, eds., *Habermas, Modernity, and Public Theology*, 23–4.

11 Gary M. Simpson, "Die Versprachlichung (und Verflüssigung?) des Sakralen," in *Habermas und die Theologie*, 158f.; also as "The Linguistification (and Liquefaction?) of the Sacred: A Theological Consideration of Jürgen Habermas's Theory of Religion," *Exploration* 7 (1989): 21–35.

12 See Peter Eicher, "Die Botschaft von der Versöhnung und die Theorie des kommunikativen Handelns," in *Habermas und die Theologie*, 199f.

13 Paul Kluke, *Die Stiftunguniversität Frankfurt am Main 1914–1932* (Frankfurt am Main, 1972); Notker Hammerstein, *Die Johann-Wolfgang-Goethe-Universität*, vol. 1 (Frankfurt am Main: Luchterhand, 1989).

14 Johann Baptist Metz, "Erinnerung," in Hermann Krings et al., eds., *Handbuch philosophischer Grundbegriffe* (München: Kösel, 1973) 2: 386–96; Metz, "Anamnetische Vernunft," in Axel Honneth, Thomas McCarthy, Claus Offe, and Albrecht Wellmer, eds., *Zwischenbetrachtungen* (Frankfurt am Main: Suhrkamp 1989), 733f.

15 Jürgen Habermas, *The Theory of Communicative Action* (Boston: Beacon Press, 1984, 1987), 2: 281ff.

16 Habermas, *The Philosophical Discourse of Modernity*, 245f.; see also my article "Die Philosophie als Platzhalter und Interpret," in Habermas, *Moralbewußtsein und kommunikatives Handeln* (Frankfurt am Main: Suhrkamp, 1983), 9–28 [*Moral Consciousness and Communicative Action* (Cambridge, Mass.: MIT Press, 1990)].

17 Jens Glebe-Möller, *A Political Dogmatic* (Philadelphia: Fortress, 1987), 102. The page numbers in the text refer to this book.

18 Trans. James Bohman (Cambridge, Mass: MIT Press, 1986) [ET of *Wissenschaftstheorie – Handlungstheorie – Fundamentale Theologie* (Düsseldorf: Patmos, 1976; Frankfurt am Main: Suhrkamp, 1978)].

19 Peukert, "Enlightenment and Theology," in Browning and Schüssler Fiorenza, eds., *Habermas, Modernity, and Public Theology*, 56.

20 Jürgen Habermas, *Die neue Unübersichtlichkeit* (Frankfurt am Main: Suhrkamp, 1985), 52.

21 Jürgen Habermas, "Individuierung durch Vergesellschaftung," in *Nachmetaphysisches Denken* (Frankfurt am Main: Suhrkamp, 1988), 187–241, esp. 192ff.

22 Habermas, *Nachmetaphysisches Denken*, 60.

23 For a more extensive treatment of this argument, see Thomas McCarthy, "Philosophical Foundations of Political Theology: Kant, Peukert and the Frankfurt School," in Leroy S. Rouner, ed., *Civil Religion and Political Theology* (Notre Dame, Ind.: University of Notre Dame Press, 1986), 23–40.

24 Peukert, "Enlightenment and Theology," 60.

25 Charles Davis, "Kommunikative Rationalität und die Grundlegung christlicher Hoffnung," in *Habermas und die Theologie*, 111.

26 Jürgen Habermas, *Eine Art Schadensabwicklung* (Frankfurt am Main: Suhrkamp, 1987), 146.

27 Albrecht Wellmer, "Wahrheit, Schein, Versöhnung. Adornos ästhetische Rettung der Modernität," in Albrecht Wellmer, *Zur Dialektik von Moderne und Postmoderne* (Frankfurt am Main: Suhrkamp, 1985), 9–47; Martin Seel, *Die Kunst der Entzweiung* (Frankfurt am Main: Suhrkamp, 1986).

28 J. Habermas, "Questions and Counterquestions," in Bernstein, ed., *Habermas and Modernity*, 192ff., here 202f.; further, Habermas, *The Philosophical Discourse of Modernity*, 204ff.

29 Charles S. Peirce, *Writings of Charles S. Peirce: A Chronological Edition, Vol. 3: 1872–1878*, ed. Max H. Fisch et al. (Bloomington, Ind.: University of Indiana Press, 1986), 3: 108.
30 Ibid., 3: 68–71.
31 Seyla Benhabib, "The Generalized and the Concrete Other," *Praxis International* 5 (1986), 406.
32 Klaus Günther, *Der Sinn für Angemessenheit. Anwendungsdiskurse in Moral und Recht* (Frankfurt am Main: Suhrkamp, 1988).
33 See the Introduction to my *Theory and Practice*, trans. John Viertel (Boston: Beacon Press, 1973), 1–40.
34 Robert Wuthnow, "Rationality and the Limits of Rational Theory," in Browning and Schüssler Fiorenza, eds., *Habermas, Modernity, and Public Theology*, 216.
35 Odo Marquard, *Abschied vom Prinzipiellen: Philosophische Studien* (Stuttgart: Reclam, 1981).
36 Fred Dallmayr, *Beyond Dogma and Despair* (Notre Dame, Ind.: University of Notre Dame Press, 1981), 220ff. and 246ff.; Dallmayr, *Twilight of Subjectivity* (Amherst: University of Massachusetts Press, 1981), 179ff. and 279ff.
37 Fred Dallmayr, *Polis and Praxis* (Cambridge, Mass.: MIT Press, 1984), 158.
38 See Fred Dallmayr, "The Discourse of Modernity: Hegel, Nietzsche, Heidegger (and Habermas)," *Praxis International* 8 (1989): 377–406; see also the discussion about *Theorie des kommunikativen Handelns* in Fred Dallmayr, *Polis and Praxis*, 224–53. Dallmayr is similarly prejudicial in "Habermas and Rationality," *Political Theory* 16 (1988): 553–79. In his response, Richard J. Bernstein remarks about Dallmayr: "Considering his hermeneutical sensitivity, his most recent discussion of Habermas comes a bit as a shock. For although he makes use of extensive citations to create the impression that the 'author' is speaking for himself, the result is a distortion of Habermas' views" (ibid., 580).
39 See Browning and Schüssler Fiorenza, eds., *Habermas, Modernity, and Public Theology*, 141. The page numbers in the text refer to this essay.
40 Habermas, *Nachmetaphysisches Denken*, 64ff.
41 See my analysis of the lifeworld in ibid., 82–104.

4

To Seek to Salvage an Unconditional Meaning Without God is a Futile Undertaking:

Reflections on a Remark of Max Horkheimer

Max Horkheimer's late philosophy, scattered throughout various notes and essays, takes the form of reflections from a damaged life. Alfred Schmidt has deciphered in them the outline of a systematic intention. His proof is an indirect one, using Horkheimer's tools as a key to unlock the door to Schopenhauer's philosophy of religion.[1] These illuminating reconstructions have impressed upon me the reasons and motives that induced Horkheimer to look to Schopenhauer in his quest for a religion that could satisfy the longing for perfect justice. Horkheimer's interest in the doctrines of Judaism and Christianity was spurred less by a concern with God as such than with the redemptive power of God's will. The injustice that comes to pass in a suffering creature should not be permitted to have the last word. At times it seems as if Horkheimer wanted to put the religious promise of redemption directly at the service of morality. At one point he explained the prohibition of images in terms of the notion that "in the Jewish religion what is important is not how things stand with God, but how they stand with men."[2] Schopenhauer's metaphysics seemed to offer a resolution of an aporia in which Horkheimer had become involved in consequence of two equally strong convictions. For him too, the critical task of philosophy consisted essentially in salvaging the truth in religion in the spirit of the

Enlightenment; nevertheless, it was clear to him that "one cannot secularize religion without giving it up."[3]

This aporia has haunted Greek philosophy like a shadow from the moment of its initial encounter with the Jewish and Christian tradition onward. In Horkheimer's case, it is made even more acute by his profound skepticism concerning reason. What for him is the essential substance of religion – morality – is no longer tied to reason. Horkheimer praises the dark writers of the bourgeoisie for having "trumpeted far and wide the impossibility of deriving from reason any fundamental argument against murder."[4] I have to admit that this remark irritates me now no less than it did almost four decades ago when I first read it. I have never been altogether convinced of the cogency of the skepticism concerning reason underlying Horkheimer's ambivalence toward religion. The idea that it is vain to strive for unconditional meaning without God betrays not just a metaphysical need; the remark is itself an instance of the metaphysics that not only philosophers but even theologians themselves must today get along without.

Before I attempt to back up this objection, I want to clarify the fundamental moral intuition that guided Horkheimer throughout his life; I will then turn to the kinship between religion and philosophy that Horkheimer never lost from sight and, finally, reveal the premises on which he based his appropriation of Schopenhauer's negative metaphysics. In what follows I draw on notes and essays that Alfred Schmidt made available to the public[5] and to whose systematic import he was first to draw attention.[6]

I

Once the rationality of the remorse experienced by a religiously tutored conscience is rejected by a secularized world, its place is taken by the moral sentiment of compassion. When Horkheimer expressly defines the good tautologically as the attempt to abolish evil, he has in view a solidarity with the suffering of vulnerable and forsaken creatures provoked by outrage against concrete injustices. The reconciling power of compassion does not stand in opposition to the galvanizing power of rebellion against a world devoid of atonement and reparation for injustice. Solidarity and justice are two sides of the same coin; hence, the ethics of compassion does not dispute the legitimacy of the morality of justice but merely frees it from the rigidity of the ethics of conscience. Otherwise the Kantian pathos expressed in Horkheimer's injunction "to proceed into the desert in spite of everything, even if hope were lost" would be incomprehensible.[7] And under the banner "necessary futility," Horkheimer does not shrink from drawing the almost Protestant conclusion: "It is true that the individual cannot change the course of the world. But if his whole life is not a gesture of wild despair that revolts against it, he will fail to realize that infinitely small, insignificant, futile, nugatory modicum of good of which he is capable as an individual."[8] The shared fate of exposure to the infinitude of an indifferent universe may awaken a feeling of solidarity in human beings, but among the community of the forsaken, the hope of solidarity and pity for one's neighbor must not undermine equal respect for everyone. Moral feelings imbued with a sense of justice are not just spontaneous impulses; they are more intuitions than impulses. In them a correct insight, in an emphatic sense of "correct," comes to expression. The positivists "have not the faintest inkling that hatred of the decent and admiration for the depraved are inverted impulses not just before the tribunal of custom, but of truth, and that they are not merely reprehensible in an ideological sense, but are objectively debased experiences and reactions."[9]

Horkheimer is so secure in his fundamental moral intuitions that he can qualify them only as "correct insights." This moral cognitivism seems to place him firmly in the Kantian camp. Nevertheless, he is so profoundly influenced by the dialectic of enlightenment that he repeatedly disputes the role Kant still accorded practical reason. What remains is only a "formalistic reason" that is no "more closely allied to morality than to immorality."[10] Material investigations alone could overcome this sterile formalism, though indeed only in a paradoxical manner. Unable to specify the good, a critical theory of society should reveal specific injustices in given cases. Because this theory, in its skepticism toward reason, no longer maintains a positive relation to the normative contents it uncovers step by step in the criticism of unjust conditions, it must borrow its normative orientations from a cultural ethos that has already been superseded – that of a metaphysically grounded theology. The latter preserves the legacy of a *substantive* reason that has since been rendered impotent.

Horkheimer is under no illusions about the vertiginous nature of this theoretical undertaking:

[Social theory] has superseded theology but has no new heaven to which it can point, not even a mundane one. Of course, social theory cannot completely efface [heaven's] traces and hence is repeatedly questioned about how it is to be attained – as though it were not precisely the discovery of social theory that the heaven to which one can point the way is no heaven.[11]

No theory could possibly accommodate itself to this Kafkaesque figure of thought, at least not without embracing an aesthetic mode of expression and becoming literature. Hence, the thoughts of the late Horkheimer circle around the idea of a theology that *must* be "displaced" by the critical and self-critical activity of reason, yet which, in its capacity as justifying morality's claim to unconditionality, *cannot* be replaced by reason. Horkheimer's late philosophy may be understood as wrestling with this dilemma and his interpretation of Schopenhauerian metaphysics as a proposal for resolving it.

In the essay entitled "Theism-Atheism," Horkheimer traces the development of the Hellenistic notion of an interrelation between theology and metaphysics up to the great metaphysical systems in which theology and natural philosophy converged. He is interested above all in the militant atheism of the eighteenth century that "was able to promote rather than to stifle interest in religion."[12] Even the materialistic antithesis to Christianity that substituted "Nature" for "God" and merely readjusted the fundamental concepts accordingly still remained caught up in the metaphysical framework of worldviews. Kant's critique of metaphysics opened the door to the mystical and messianic currents that, from Baader and Schelling to Hegel and Marx, found their way into philosophy. Horkheimer was aware of the theological current in Marxist theory from the beginning: with the idea of a just society, the Enlightenment opened up the prospect of a new beyond in the here and now; the spirit of the Gospel was now to reach worldly fulfillment through the march of history.

The secular sublation [*Aufhebung*] of ontotheology by the philosophy of history has profoundly equivocal implications. On the one hand, philosophy becomes disguised theology and salvages the latter's essential content. The very meaning of atheism itself ensures the enduring relevance of theism:

Only those who employed the word in a derogatory sense understood it as the opposite of religion. Those who professed atheism at a time when religion still had power were wont to identify themselves more sincerely with the theistic precept of devotion to one's neighbor and other creatures as such than most of the adherents and fellow travelers of the various religious confessions.[13]

On the other hand, philosophy can recover the idea of the unconditioned only in the medium of a reason that has in the interim sacrificed the infinite on the altar of historical contingency and has abjured the unconditioned. A reason that can appeal to no authority higher than that of the sciences is a naturalized faculty that has regressed to intelligence in the service of pure self-affirmation; it measures itself by the yardstick of functional contributions and technical successes, and not by a mode of validity that transcends space and time: "With God dies eternal truth."[14] *In the wake of* the Enlightenment, the truth in religion can be salvaged only in a way that annihilates truth. A critical theory that sees itself as the "successor" to theology finds itself in this unhappy predicament because everything to do with morality ultimately derives from theology.

II

The rational sublation of theology and its essential contents: how can this still be accomplished in the present day, in the light of the irreversible critique of metaphysics, without destroying the import of religious doctrines or of reason itself? With this question Horkheimer, the pessimistic materialist, appeals to Schopenhauer, the pessimistic idealist. On Horkheimer's surprising interpretation, Schopenhauer's enduring importance lies in the fact that his thoroughgoing negativism salvages the "spirit of the Gospels." According to Horkheimer, Schopenhauer accomplished the improbable feat of providing an atheistic justification of the morality underlying theology, and thus of preserving religion in the absence of God.

In the world as will and representation, Horkheimer discerns, first, the sterile Darwinian operation of instrumental reason degraded to a tool of self-preservation, which – up to and including a globally objectifying scientific intellect – is dominated by a blind and indefatigable will to life that pits one subject against another. On the other hand, precisely this reflection on the abysmally negative ground of being is supposed to awaken in subjects who seek remorselessly to dominate one another some inkling of their *common* fate and an awareness that all manifestations of life are pervaded by an *identical* will:

> If the realm of appearances, sensible reality, is not the work of posi-
> tive divine power, an expression of inherently good, eternal Being, but
> of a will that affirms itself in everything finite, that is mirrored in a
> distorted fashion in multiplicity, and yet that remains at a profound
> level identical, then everyone has reason to view himself as one with
> all others, not with their specific motives, but with their entanglement
> in delusion and guilt, their drivenness, joy and decline. The life and
> fate of the founder of Christianity becomes a model, no longer based
> on commands but on insight into the inner constitution of the world.[15]

What fascinated Horkheimer in Schopenhauer is the prospect of a metaphysical justification of morality through insight into the constitution of the world as a whole, yet in such a way that this insight is at the same time directed against central assumptions of metaphysics and coheres with postmetaphysical skepticism concerning reason. Negative metaphysics upholds the distinction between essence and appearance only with an inversion of the order of priority between them – inverted Platonism. This in turn grounds the expectation that insight into the "pitiless structure of infinitude" could produce "a community of the forsaken." However, Horkheimer is aware of the shadow of performative self-contradiction that has haunted all negative metaphysics since Schopenhauer and Nietzsche. Even if we prescind from epistemological misgivings about intuitive, bodily access to the thing-in-itself, it remains mysterious how the turning of the irrational world-will against itself that constrains it to continual reflection will come about: "The metaphysics of the irrational will as the essence of the world must lead to reflection on the problematic of truth."[16] In Schmidt's formulation of the dilemma, "If the essence of the world is irrational, then that cannot remain incidental to the truth claim of precisely this thesis."[17] In the light of this result, the statement that it is futile to seek to salvage unconditional meaning without God can also be understood as a criticism of Schopenhauer, as a critique of the "last great philosophical attempt to rescue the essential core of Christianity."[18]

In the final analysis, Horkheimer's ambiguous formulations vacillate between Schopenhauer's negative-metaphysical justification of morality and a return to the faith of his forefathers. This unresolved argumentative impasse leads me to reexamine the premise from which Horkheimer's late philosophy begins: that "formalistic" reason, or the procedural reason that remains under conditions of post-metaphysical thought, is equally indifferent to morality and immorality. As far as I can discern, Horkheimer's skeptical assertion rests primarily on the contemporary experience of Stalinism and on a conceptual argument that presupposes the ontological concept of truth.

III

Horkheimer's thought is influenced even more than Adorno's by the harrowing historical fact that the ideals of freedom, solidarity, and justice deriving from practical reason, which inspired the French Revolution and were reappropriated in Marx's critique of society, led not to socialism but to barbarism under the guise of socialism:

> The vision of instituting justice and freedom in the world which under-lay Kant's thought has been transformed into the mobilization of nations. With each revolt that followed in the wake of the great revolution in France, it seems, the humanistic elements atrophied while nationalism thrived. In this century it was socialism itself that orchestrated the supreme farce of perverting the pledge to humanity into an intransigent cult of the state. . . . What Lenin and the majority of his comrades aspired to before assuming power was a free and just society. In reality they prepared the way for a totalitarian bureaucracy under whose sway there was no more freedom than in the tsarist empire. That the new China is entering on a phase of barbarism is plain to see.[19]

From this experience Horkheimer drew consequences for the reconstruction of the architectonic of reason announced in the concept of "instrumental reason." There is no longer any difference between the operation of the understanding in the service of subjective self-assertion, which imposes its categories on everything and transforms it into an object, and reason as the faculty of ideas whose place understanding has usurped. Indeed, the ideas themselves have been caught up in the dynamic of reification; elevated to absolute ends, they retain merely a functional significance for *other* ends. But by exhausting the

supply of ideas in this way, every claim that points beyond instrumental rationality loses its transcending power; truth and morality
forfeit their unconditional meaning.

Thinking that is sensitive to historical changes, even down to its
fundamental concepts, submits itself to the tribunal of new experience. Thus, it is not inappropriate to ask whether the bankruptcy of
state socialism that has in the interim become apparent does not offer
other lessons, for this bankruptcy is partly the doing of ideas that the
regime, while distancing itself from them ever further, misused for
the purposes of its own legitimation because – which is more important – it *had* to appeal to them. A system that collapsed despite its
brutal Orwellian apparatus of oppression because social conditions
eloquently contradicted everything prefigured by its legitimating
ideas, manifestly cannot *dispose of the inner logic of these ideas as it
wishes*. In the ideas of the constitutionally embodied republican
tradition, however egregiously abused, there persists the element of
existing reason that resisted the "dialectic of enlightenment" by elud-
ing the leveling gaze of the negative philosophy of history.

The controversy surrounding this thesis could be resolved only by
recourse to material analyses. As a consequence, I will limit myself
to the conceptual argument that Horkheimer develops from the
critique of instrumental reason.

Horkheimer's assertion that the difference between reason and
understanding has *become obsolete* in the course of the world-
historical process still presupposed, in contrast to contemporary post-
structuralism, that we can *recall* the emphatic concept of reason. The
critical import of "instrumental reason" is first thrown into relief by
this act of recollection. And through anamnetic retrieval of the
substantive reason of religious and metaphysical worldviews, we can
reassure ourselves of the unconditionality that concepts such as truth
and morality once carried with them before they succumbed to
positivistic and functionalistic disintegration. An Absolute or Unconditional becomes accessible to philosophy only together with justification of the world as a whole, and hence only as metaphysics. But
philosophy remains true to its metaphysical beginnings only as long
as it attempts "to imitate positive theology" and proceeds on the
assumption that cognizing reason rediscovers itself in the rationally
structured world or itself actually confers a rational structure on
nature and history. As soon as the world "in its essence, by contrast,
does *not* of necessity cohere with the spirit, philosophical confidence
in the being of truth dissipates completely. Then truth is henceforth

sublated only in transient human beings themselves and becomes as transient as they are."[20]

It never occurred to Horkheimer that there might be a difference between "instrumental" and "formal" reason. Moreover, he unceremoniously assimilated procedural reason – which no longer makes the validity of its results dependent on the rational organization of the world but on the rationality of procedures through which it solves its problems – to instrumental reason. Horkheimer assumes that there cannot be truth without an Absolute, without a world-transcending power "in which truth is sublated." Without ontological anchoring, the concept of truth is exposed to the inner-worldly contingencies of mortal men and their changing situations; without it, truth is no longer an idea but merely a weapon in the struggle of life. Human knowledge, including moral insight, can lay claim to truth, he believes, only if it judges itself in terms of relations between it and what is as these relations are manifested to the divine intelligence alone. In contrast to this strangely traditional conception, in the final section I will argue for a modern alternative – a concept of communicative reason that enables us to recover the meaning of the unconditioned without recourse to metaphysics. But first we must clarify the true motive that causes Horkheimer to hold fast to the classical concept of truth as *adaequatio intellectus ad rem*.

Decisive for Horkheimer's persistence in maintaining an ontological anchoring of truth are the ethical reflections he attributes to Schopenhauer: only insight into the identity of all life, into a unitary ground of being, even if it be irrational, in which all individual appearances are brought into harmony with one another, "can ground solidarity with all creatures long before death."[21] The unified thought of metaphysics renders plausible why it should be that the effort to overcome egoism would find a sympathetic response in the constitution of the world. For this reason alone, unity takes precedence over multiplicity for philosophers, the unconditional occurs only in the singular, and the one God has greater importance for Jews and Christians than the multiple deities of antiquity. It is the peculiar fate of bourgeois culture that individuals entrench themselves in their particularity and thereby reduce individualism to a falsehood. Horkheimer so emphatically regards this societal state of nature of competitive society as the fundamental problem of morality that for him justice and solidarity become synonymous with "renouncing the self-assertion of the isolated ego." Egoism has congealed to such an extent into an inverted condition of things that the transition from self-love to devotion to others is unthinkable without metaphysical assurance of the prior unity of an unfathomable world-will that provokes us to insight into a possible solidarity of the destitute:

> Schopenhauer drew the necessary consequences: the insight into the baseness of one's own life which cannot be separated from the suffering of other creatures is correct; the identification with those who suffer, with man and animal, is correct, the renunciation of self-love, of the drive to individual well-being as the ultimate goal; and the induction after death into the general, the non-personal, the nothing is desirable.[22]

The individuated will is base only when it turns itself against others; it becomes good when, through compassion, it recognizes its true identity with all other beings.

IV

Already in *The Dialectic of Enlightenment* Horkheimer credits de Sade and Nietzsche with the recognition that "after the formalization of reason, compassion still remained, so to speak, as the sensual consciousness of the identity of the general and the particular, as naturalized mediation."[23] On the Schopenhauerian interpretation, of course, compassion cannot assume the role of dialectical *mediation* between individual and society, between equal respect for all and the solidarity of each with all. Here it is solely a matter of the abstract self-overcoming of individuality, of the dissolution of the individual in an all-encompassing oneness. But with this the very idea in which the moral substance of Christianity consists is abrogated. Those who at the Last Judgment come, one after the other, before the eyes of God as unrepresentable individuals stripped of the mantle of worldly goods and honors – and hence as equals – in the expectation of receiving a fair judgment, experience themselves as *fully individuated beings* who must give an account of their life histories in full responsibility for their actions. Together with this idea, however, the profound intuition that the bond between solidarity and justice must not be severed must also be given up.

Admittedly, in this respect Horkheimer does not follow Schopenhauer without misgivings. His interpretation of the Ninety-first Psalm reveals his struggle to overcome a certain dissonance. The doctrine of the individual soul, he writes, has an additional significance in Judaism, one unadulterated by the expectation of an afterlife:

> The idea of continued existence signifies in the first instance, not the after-life, but the identification with the nation so crassly distorted by modern nationalism, which has its prehistory in the Bible. By conducting his life in accordance with the Torah, by spending days, months, years in obedience to the Law, the individual becomes so much one with others despite personal differences that after his death he continues to exist through those who survive him, in their observance of tradition, of love for the family and the tribe, in the expectation that at some time things may still become better in the world. ... Not unlike the figure of Jesus in Christianity, Judaism *as a whole* bore witness to redemption.[24]

Horkheimer tries to circumvent the problem of superseding the individual, of repudiating inalienable individuality, by changing the question. The issue is not whether the kingdom of the Messiah is of this world but whether the fundamental moral intuition of Judaism and Christianity to which Horkheimer unwaveringly adheres can ultimately be adequately explained without reference to the unrestricted *individuation* possible in a *universal* confederation.

The moral impulse of unwillingness to resign oneself to the force of circumstances that have the effect of isolating the individual and to secure the happiness and power of one person only at the cost of the misfortune and powerlessness of another – this impulse confirms Horkheimer in the view that the reconciling potential of solidarity with those who suffer can be realized only if individuals renounce themselves as individuals. He fails to see that the danger of a nationalistic distortion of the identificatory bond with the nation arises precisely at the moment when false solidarity permits individuals to be subsumed into the collectivity. Unified metaphysical thought – however negatively accented – transposes solidarity, which has its proper place in linguistic intersubjectivity, communication, and individuating socialization, into the identity of an underlying essence, the undifferentiated negativity of the world-will.

Quite a different, dialectical unity is produced in communication in which the structure of language inscribes the gap between I and Thou. The structure of linguistic intersubjectivity makes harmony between the integration of autonomy and devotion to others possible for us – in other words, a reconciliation that does not efface differences. Horkheimer is by no means deaf to this promise of reconciliation inherent in language itself. At one point he puts it trenchantly: "Language, whether it wants to or not, must lay claim to truth."[25] He also recognizes that we have to take into account the pragmatic dimension of language use, for the context-transcending truth-claim of speech cannot be grasped from the blinkered perspective of a semantics that reduces utterances to propositions: "Truth in speech is not properly predicated of detached, naked judgments, as though printed on a piece of paper, but of the conduct of the speaker toward the world that is expressed in the judgment and concentrates itself in this place."[26] What Horkheimer has in mind is clearly the theological tradition, extending from Augustine through logos mysticism to radical Protestantism, that appeals to the originary character of the divine Word and to language as the medium of the divine message to man: "But theological metaphysics is in the right against positivism, because no proposition can avoid raising the impossible claim, not merely to an anticipated result, to success, as positivism, maintains, but to truth in the proper sense, regardless of whether the speaker reflects on it or not."[27] Prayer, in which the believer seeks contact with God, would lose its categorial difference from incantation and regress to the level of magic if we confused the illocutionary force of our assertions with their perlocutionary effects, as does the unrealizable program of linguistic nominalism.

But these insights remain sporadic. Horkheimer fails to treat them as clues to a language-pragmatical explanation of the *unconditional* meaning associated with *unavoidable* truth claims. His skepticism toward reason is so thoroughgoing that he can no longer see room for communicative action in the world as it is now constituted: "Today talk has become stale and those who do not want to listen are not altogether wrong. . . . Speaking has had its day. Indeed so has action, at least insofar as it was once related to speech."[28]

V

His pessimistic diagnosis of the times is not the only reason that Horkheimer refrains from seriously entertaining the question of how something we accomplish on a daily basis – orienting our action to context-transcending validity claims – is possible. In fact, a profane answer to this question, such as the one proposed by Peirce, for instance, could not have *sufficiently* satisfied Horkheimer's metaphysical need for religion.

Horkheimer equated Kant's formalistic reason with instrumental reason. But Peirce reinterprets Kantian formalism in the direction of a pragmatics of language and construes reason in procedural terms. The process of sign interpretation achieves self-awareness at the level of argumentation. Peirce now shows how this nonquotidian form of communication is commensurate with the "unconditional meaning" of truth and of context-transcending validity claims in general. He conceives of truth as the redeemability of a truth claim under the communicative conditions of an ideal community of interpreters – that is, one extended ideally in social space and historical time. The counterfactual appeal to an *unlimited* communication community of this kind replaces the moment of infinitude or the supratemporal character of "unconditionality" with the idea of an open yet goal-directed process of interpretation that transcends the boundaries of social space *from within* from the perspective of an existence situated *in the world. In time,* learning processes are to form an arch bridging all temporal distance; *in the world,* the conditions we assume are at least sufficiently fulfilled in every argument are to be realized. We are intuitively aware that we cannot rationally *convince* anyone, not even ourselves, of something if we do not accept as our common point of departure that all voices that are at all relevant should be heard, that the best arguments available given the current state of our knowledge should be expressed, and that only the unforced force of the better argument should determine the "yes" and "no" responses of participants.

The tension between the intelligible realm and the realm of phenomena is thereby shifted to general presuppositions of communication, which – despite their ideal and only approximately realizable content – participants must in every case actually accept if they wish to thematize a controversial truth claim. The idealizing force of these transcending anticipations penetrates into the very heart of everyday communicative praxis, for even the most fleeting speech-act-offer, the most conventional "yes" or "no," *point* to potential reasons, and hence to the ideally extended audience they must convince if they are valid. The ideal moment of unconditionality is deeply rooted in factual processes of communication because validity claims are Janus faced: as universal, they outstrip every given context; at the same time, they must be raised and gain acceptance here and now if they are to sustain an agreement capable of coordinating action. In communicative action, we orient ourselves to validity claims that we can raise only as a matter of fact in the context of *our* language, of *our* form of life, whereas the redeemability implicitly co-posited points beyond the provinciality of the given historical context. Whoever employs a language with a view to reaching understanding lays himself open to a transcendence from within. He is left without any choice because he masters the structure of language through the intentionality of the spoken word. Linguistic intentionality outstrips subjects but without *subjugating* them.

Postmetaphysical thought differs from religion in that it recovers the meaning of the unconditional without recourse to God or an Absolute. Horkheimer's dictum would have been justified only if by "unconditional meaning" he had meant something different from the notion of unconditionality that also belongs to the meaning of truth as one of its moments. The significance of unconditionality is not to be confused with an unconditional meaning that offers consolation. On the premises of postmetaphysical thought, philosophy cannot provide a substitute for the consolation whereby religion invests unavoidable suffering and unrecompensed injustice, the contingencies of need, loneliness, sickness, and death, with new significance and teaches us to bear them. But even today philosophy can explicate the moral point of view from which we can judge something impartially as just or unjust; to this extent, communicative reason is by no means equally indifferent to morality and immorality. However, it is altogether a different matter to provide a motivating response to the question of why we should follow our moral insights or why we should be moral at all. In *this* respect, it may perhaps be said that to seek to salvage an unconditional meaning without God is a futile undertaking, for it belongs to the peculiar dignity of philosophy to maintain adamantly that no validity claim can have cognitive import unless it is vindicated before the tribunal of justificatory discourse.

Translated by Ciaran P. Cronin

Notes

1   Alfred Schmidt, *Die Wahrheit im Gewande der Lüge* (Munich, 1986); "Religion as Trug und als metaphysisches Bedürfnis," *Quatuor Coronati* (1988), pp. 87ff.; "Aufklärung und Mythos im Werk Max Horkheimers,"

in A. Schmidt and N. Altwicker (eds.), *Max Horkheimer heute* (Frankfurt, 1986), pp. 180ff.
2 Max Horkheimer, "Gespräch mit Helmut Gumnior," *Gesammelte Schriften* [henceforth cited as GS] (Frankfurt, 1985–91), 7: 387.
3 GS, 7: 393.
4 Max Horkheimer and Theodor W. Adorno, *Dialectic of Enlightenment*, trans. J. Cumming (New York, 1972), p. 118.
5 Max Horkheimer, *Notizen 1950 bis 1969* (Frankfurt, 1974).
6 This holds above all for the philosophical articles that Alfred Schmidt already included in the appendix to the German edition of *The Critique of Instrumental Reason* (*Zur Kritik der instrumentellen Vernunft* [Frankfurt, 1967], pp. 177ff.).
7 Horkheimer, *Notizen*, p. 93.
8 Horkheimer, *Notizen*, p. 184.
9 Horkheimer, *Notizen*, p. 102.
10 Horkheimer and Adorno, *Dialectic*, p. 118.
11 Horkheimer, *Notizen*, p. 61.
12 GS, 7: 178.
13 "Theismus-Atheismus," GS, 7: 185ff.
14 GS, 7: 184.
15 "Religion und Philosophie," GS, 7: 193.
16 "Die Aktualität Schopenhauers," GS, 7: 136.
17 Schmidt, *Die Wahrheit im Gewande der Lüge*, p. 121.
18 "Religion und Philosophie," GS, 7: 191.
19 "Die Aktualität Schopenhauers," GS, 7: 138f.
20 GS, 7: 135f.
21 "Schopenhauers Denken," GS, 7: 252.
22 "Pessimismus Heute," GS, 7: 227f.
23 Horkheimer and Adorno, *Dialectic*, p. 101.
24 "Psalm 91," GS, 7: 210.
25 Horkheimer, *Notizen*, p. 26.
26 Horkheimer, *Notizen*, p. 172.
27 "Die Aktualität Schopenhauers," GS, 7: 138.
28 Horkheimer, *Notizen*, p. 26.

5

Communicative Freedom and Negative Theology

Questions for Michael Theunissen

The quiet radicality of Michael Theunissen's thought derives from his simultaneous openness to Kierkegaard and to Marx. Theunissen responds to the two creative minds who – more radically than all others – were marked by their engagement with the speculative thought of Hegel. This is why he has paid special attention to the two styles of thought which have brought Kierkegaard and Marx back to philosophical life in our century: existential ontology and Hegelian Marxism. He engages with both traditions by returning to their original points of inspiration: in his view, the insights of the authentic Kierkegaard and a critically appropriated Marx are superior to those of Heidegger and Sartre, or Horkheimer and Adorno.[1] In this project Theunissen is aided by a turn towards the theory of communication which he made early on in his career. He emphasizes the relevance of the second person – the other in the role of 'Thou' – in contrast to a subject–object relation defined by the attitudes of first and third person.

The dialogical encounter with an other whom I address, and whose answer lies beyond my control, first opens the intersubjective space in which the individual can become an authentic self. Theunissen developed his philosophy of dialogue through a critical engagement with the transcendental theory of intersubjectivity, as developed from Husserl to Sartre. It is inspired not just by Buber's 'theology of the between', but also draws directly on theological motifs. Indeed, Theunissen understands that 'middle' of the intersubjective space which the dialogical encounter discloses, and which in turn enables self and other to become themselves through dialogue, as the 'kingdom of God' which precedes and founds the existing sphere of subjectivity. Referring to Luke 17: 21 – 'the kingdom of God is among you' – Theunissen declares: 'It exists *between* the human beings who are called to it, as a present future.' Throughout his career, Theunissen has tried to retrieve the content of this crucial statement in *philosophical* terms. For,

> presumably the reality as which the between discloses itself to dialogical thinking in a theological perspective is the only side of the kingdom of God that philosophy can catch a glimpse of at all: the side not of 'grace', but of the 'will'. The will to dialogical self-becoming belongs to the striving after the kingdom of God, whose future coming is promised in the present love of human beings for one another.[2]

Later in his career, Theunissen sought to integrate this theological motif into a critical social theory with the aid of the concept of 'communicative freedom'. His aim was to make Kierkegaard compatible with Marx. He has not evaded the decision which this project eventually required: the choice between a materialistic and a theological reading of reconciliation. He has always preferred the proleptic appearance of an *eschaton* which can instil *confidence* into the present to a rationally *fortified* transcendence from within. But, in his view, even this option can be philosophically grounded. This is the claim that I would like to test in what follows. Theunissen finds the possibility of such a grounding in Kierkegaard, and he seems to find it, in particular, in an aspect of Fichte's theory which was taken up by Kierkegaard. Of course, Theunissen has no wish to hide behind the authority of the author of *The Sickness unto Death*. But Kierkegaard's arguments do provide the impetus behind Theunissen's negativistic grounding of an authentic selfhood.

I would first like to outline the claim that essential contents of the Christian gospel of salvation can be justified under the conditions of postmetaphysical thinking. I will then discuss the arguments which Theunissen employs in his effort to satisfy this claim by pursuing 'the paths of philosophical thought which are still viable today'. My critical queries do not affect my sense of solidarity with a remarkable enterprise, one with which I feel closely allied in its practical motivation and intentions.

I

In the history of Western thought since Augustine, Christianity has entered into many kinds of symbiotic relationship with the metaphysical tradition stemming from Plato. Along with theologians such as Jürgen Moltmann and Johann Baptist Metz,[3] Theunissen has sought to retrieve the original eschatological content of a Christianity freed from its Hellenistic shell. The kernel thus retrieved is a radically historical mode of thought which is incompatible with essentialist conceptions: 'It is the domination of what is past over what is to come which results in the compulsive character of a reality in need of salvation. This reality takes the form of a universal pattern of compulsion because, within it, the future is constantly overwhelmed by the past.'[4] In Theunissen this sentence has a precise meaning which extends beyond Adorno's 'negative dialectics':

> If it is the domination of the past which causes human beings to sink into the helplessness of an incapacity to act, then what awakens them from this helplessness is the liberating action of God. Existence within time, which the metaphysical tradition deriving from Plato viewed under the negative aspect of the mutable, acquires the positive shape of the alterable.[5]

However, what distinguishes Theunissen's position from that of theologians with similar aims is the claim that he can achieve their common goal with non-theological means. Indeed, Theunissen borrows these means from the basic repertoire of metaphysical concepts bequeathed by the very Platonism which is to be overcome. In so doing, he abandons the careful distinction between those aspects of 'grace' under which the kingdom of God is disclosed only to theologians, and of 'will' under which it also appears to philosophers. He seems confident that he can close the gap between the appeal to a reality experienced in faith, and the power to convince of philosophical reasons. What is more, he thinks he can do so with arguments.

After the catastrophes of our century, Benjamin's intuition that the bad continuity of all previous history must be broken apart – the cry of the tortured creature, that 'everything must be different' – undoubtedly has a more than merely suggestive force. Today we are confronted on all sides by the regressions which the collapse of the Soviet empire has triggered. In the face of these phenomena, the impulse to *rebel* against the domination of the past over the future,[6] even the imperative to burst the shackles of the fatal return of the same, seems to require no extensive justification: 'Benjamin has evoked the unutterable sadness of a history which has congealed into nature. History would first come into being only if time itself could become other than it is.'[7] But what sense are we to make of such an expectation? Do we regard it as the prospect of an event yet to occur, as trust in a promised reversal, or as hope for the success of an enterprise which enjoys divine favour, perhaps even grace? Or is the semantic potential of the anticipation of salvation intended only to hold open a *dimension*, one which, even in profane times, offers us a criterion by which to orient ourselves towards what is better *in given circumstances*, and from which we can draw encouragement?

The hope that one's own activity is not a fortiori meaningless can be wrested from pessimism, and indeed despair, with more or less valid reasons. But such rationally motivated encouragement should not be confused with an existential confidence which emerges out of the totalized scepticism of a despair which is turned against itself. The *hope* that 'everything within time will be different' must be distinguished from the *faith* that 'time itself will be different'. The ambiguous formula of a 'becoming other of time' [*Anderswerden der Zeit*] conceals this difference between trust in an eschatological turning of the world, and the profane expectation that our praxis in the world, despite everything, may help to bring about a shift towards a better state of things. On this side of a *spes fidei* nourished by the Kierkegaardian dialectics of despair, there is room for fallible hope, instructed by a sceptical, but non-defeatist conception of reason. This *docta spes* is not to be despised, even though it can sometimes be devastated. Presumably, Theunissen would not deny the distinction, but he would hold fast to the task of showing philosophically why profane hope must be anchored in eschatological hope.

In his most recent publication, Theunissen names three paths of philosophical thought which he regards as still viable today. Philosophy can entrust itself with the critical appropriation of the history of metaphysics as a whole; it can make a contribution to reflection on the specialized sciences, and it can even retrieve, from its post-metaphysical vantage point, metaphysical contents of the tradition which resist scientific objectification. According to this programme, philosophy first follows the path of historical self-reflection, in order to secure its hold on the concepts which it then unfolds systematically in its passage through the sciences, and in the space beyond them.[8] Thus, the themes which concern Theunissen from a historical standpoint already reveal a systematic intention. Under the title 'communicative freedom' he analyses the relation between subjectivity and intersubjectivity in an exploration of Hegel's *Logic*. And with one eye on the *proleptic future* of a Christian promise of salvation which reaches into the present, he analyses the forgetfulness of time characteristic of metaphysical thought from Parmenides through to Hegel. From both perspectives Theunissen traces the ontologization of theology, in other words a Hellenization of Christianity which covers over the redemptive content of radically historical thinking. Like Heidegger, Theunissen is striving for a deconstruction of the history of metaphysics. But the aim he has in mind is not the 'archaeological' one of leaping out of modernity back towards a time before Jesus and Socrates. Theunissen's goal, rather, is a philosophically grounded negative theology. The task of this theology is to recall a disintegrated modernity from its dispersal, re-sensitizing it to a message of salvation which has become unintelligible.

II

Theunissen applies a hypothesis to Hegel's *Logic*, which – in its own way – summarizes the history of Western metaphysics. It is one which he derives from post-Hegelian philosophy: 'Hegel bases his whole logic on the hypothesis that everything which exists can only be itself in relation, and – ultimately – *as* the relation to its other.'[9] Theunissen opposes the being-for-itself of subjectivity to this self-relation which realizes itself in the relation to the other. True selfhood expresses itself as communicative freedom – as being-with-*oneself*-in-the-other; love – being-with-oneself-in-the-*other* – stands in a complementary relation to this. The interrelation – or better, coincidence – of freedom and love defines the unimpaired intersubjectivity of a relation of reciprocal recognition. In such a relation one partner is not the limit of the other's freedom, but the very condition of the other's successful selfhood. And the communicative freedom of one individual cannot be complete without the realized freedom of all others. This notion of a solidaristic and non-compulsive form of socialization enables Theunissen to give Hegel's concrete universal a dialogical structure, one which can be turned against Hegel himself with critical intent. 'Abstraction' then comes to mean an 'indifference towards what is other' which neutralizes the 'relation to the other'. Because it impedes communicative freedom, this indifference comes in turn to signify domination. Read from the standpoint of a theory of communication, Hegel's dialectic acquires a new meaning as a critique of *domination*.

Theunissen argues with Hegel against Hegel. He highlights the passages where Hegel deviates from the path of a dialectical investigation of the 'praxis of speaking with one another', and neglects the obvious dimension of the pragmatics of language for the sake of a logical analysis of the 'mere judgement or proposition'.[10] Hegel's logical and semantic restriction of his investigation bolsters the arrogance of the model of reflection, which privileges the being-with-oneself of the epistemic self-relation over the relation to the other. Whereas communicative freedom would foster the reciprocal recognition of difference and otherness, the reflection model enforces unity and totalization.[11]

Theunissen also opposes the affirmative traits of the theodicy concealed in dialectical logic, with its equation of the real and the rational. Hegel's concept of the 'untrue' effaces the difference between the contentless, and that which has not yet developed. Theunissen seeks to restore this difference with the aid of Marx's distinction between presentation and critique. The dissolution of objective illusion need not always disclose the truth of a new positivity; it often functions destructively, in the sense that it unmasks the truth *about* something.[12] Significantly, this aspect of his thought already highlights what Theunissen, despite all his criticisms, is unwilling to criticize in Hegel – the concept of the absolute.

There is a plausible claim to be made that Hegel's concept of determinate negation assumes a unity of presentation [*Darstellung*] and critique which blunts the critical edge of presentation. But Theunissen reduces this to a merely methodological question, even though, in Hegel, the unity of presentation and critique is grounded in the substantive assumption that the world-process as a whole has a logical structure. Theunissen does not touch on this metaphysical core of the problem. He does not consider the difficulty that no pathogenesis of history can arise from the orthogenesis of nature, if the historical process has the same logical form as that of events in nature. His critique of Hegel does not extend to Hegel's *totalization* of being-with-oneself-in-the-other, which assumes that the world *as a whole* is communicatively constituted. The idea of the unity of the relation to self and the relation to the other guides the *whole movement* of Hegel's logic, and extends to embrace a reality which is understood *entirely* in intersubjective terms. This idea is in no sense restricted to the sphere of interpersonal relations. Theunissen accepts this, although he stresses that reading the *Logic* as a universal theory of communication should make clear that 'the structure it reveals finds its appropriate realization only in the relation of human subjects to each other'.[13] In other words, Theunissen does not dissent from the metaphysical assumption that the basic structure of being-with-oneself-in-the-other, which is derived from the process of dialogical understanding, extends beyond the horizon of the lifeworld to embrace the world as a whole.

This is because he is convinced that every interpersonal relation is embedded in a relation to the radically Other, which precedes the relation to the concrete Other. This radically Other embodies an absolute freedom which we must presuppose in order to explain how our communicative freedom is possible at all: 'for nothing can be absolute unless it can release the other out of itself, in such a way that the freedom of the other is also its own freedom from and towards itself.'[14] This conception can be traced back to elements of Jewish and Protestant mysticism, which have been passed down through Swabian Pietism: God's freedom is confirmed by the fact that He is able to produce an equally free alter ego out of Himself. In handing over to human beings the freedom to fall short of – and to struggle to achieve – selfhood through their own efforts, God withdraws from the world. God is present in the history of human communication only as an enabling and guiding structure of reconciliation – and indeed in the form of a promise, the 'anticipatory' present of a fulfilled future.[15]

As this shows, a systematic appropriation of the history of metaphysics can reveal problematic issues which are perhaps not yet outdated. But can it abolish our distance from the solutions which were proposed in the language of metaphysics? Even a reading of the 'Logic of the Notion' in terms of a theory of communication can, at best, make us *familiar* with the idea that the communicative freedom of being-with-oneself-in-the-other presupposes the absolute freedom of the radically Other. In the last analysis, it still remains undecided how this potential contained in the structure of undistorted communication is to be understood. Should we see it as an idealizing excess, which requires an ability to transcend the given context on the part of those involved in communicative action *themselves*? Or should we view it as the irruption of an anticipatory event of communicative liberation, which demands *self-abandonment* on the part of those left to make sense of their own freedom? If we assume that God has withdrawn into the transcendent moment of the structure of linguistic understanding, and has entrusted the historical process to His creatures, who are condemned to communicative freedom, then the very myth of a self-limiting God must eventually succumb to their secularizing labours. But if God *remains* the only guarantee within history that the ceaseless, nature-bound cycles of history – dominated, as it is, by the past – can be broken, then the notion of an absolute which is presupposed in every successful act of mutual understanding is left without an adequate philosophical explanation. This task cannot be carried out by means of a destruction of the history of metaphysics.

III

This is why Theunissen tries to achieve a postmetaphysically oriented grounding of the metaphysical content of communicative freedom. He unfolds his argument with reference to the text *The Sickness unto Death*.

(1) First of all, Theunissen distinguishes his 'negativistic' procedure from a 'normativistic' one. In modern times, since the abandonment of the concepts of substance and essence which anchored what ought to be in the order of things, the architectonics of reason has replaced objective teleology. This means that normative contents can only be derived reconstructively from the necessary subjective conditions for the objective validity of our experiences and judgements. They can no longer be derived ontologically from being itself. Of course, the shift from the paradigm of consciousness to the paradigm of mutual understanding achieved by the pragmatics of

language has given yet another new direction to the investigation of normatively significant transcendental conditions. Now it is the fact of successful intersubjective communication which requires explanation. In the general and unavoidable pragmatic presuppositions of communication, we discover the counter-factual content of idealizations which all subjects must accept in so far as they orient their action towards validity-claims at all. The non-arbitrary character of the *broadly* normative content of the unavoidable presuppositions of communication can be established neither ontologically, nor epistemologically. In other words, it cannot be shown with reference to the purposive character of being, or with reference to the rational endowments of subjectivity. It can only be made plausible through the lack of alternatives to a practice in which communicatively socialized subjects always already find themselves engaged. I have adopted this formal-pragmatic approach in my own work, in order to reveal a rational potential in the validity-basis of action oriented towards mutual understanding. This rational potential can provide the normative basis for a critical theory of society.[16]

Theunissen rejects this 'normativism', but not because he detects in it the metaphysical trace of essential determinations and objective teleology.[17] On the contrary, the 'negativism' which is supposed to guide his own procedure shifts the normative content back into the ontical domain, albeit through an inversion of the 'ought' inherent in being. Whereas the logical operation of negation applies to the affirmative validity-claim which a second person raises for his utterance, 'ontic negativity' is an intrinsic property of whatever we evaluate negatively: 'What we mean by the "negative" here is that with which we do not agree, or that which we do not [cannot] will to exist. In this [ontological] sense, it ought not to be.'[18] Admittedly, the negativity of that which should not be, or the objectively untrue, is no longer related, like objective teleology, to entities in the world, or the cosmos of beings as a whole. In line with an inverted philosophy of history, the constitution of the historical world in which human beings live and suffer becomes negative. The negativity of the constitution of being is the *experienced* negativity of a lifeworld or life history. For this reason, the investigation is supposed to begin from the 'negativity of the existing world' and derive the yardstick of critique from this negativity. Theunissen's justification for this 'negativistic' procedure is that the pervasive pathology of the prevailing state of the world has long since corrupted the criteria for an *inno-*

cent distinction between health and sickness, truth and untruth, idea and appearance. Once the sickness of the healthy is revealed, then any diagnosis carried out in the light of an unquestioned assumption of normality falls prey to the hermeneutics of suspicion.

(2) Beginning from Marx and Kierkegaard, there are ways of trying to demonstrate negatively that communicative freedom harbours a potential for betterment and reconciliation. One can point to the social *alienation* experienced in societies that have undergone capitalist rationalization, and the existential *despair* of the isolated individual in a secularized modernity. To a large extent, Theunissen has left the first path for his pupils to follow;[19] he has concentrated on working out an argument which Kierkegaard introduces for the identity of belief in God and being-a-self.[20] The reconstruction of this line of argument characterizes the phenomenon of despair in the first instance as ontic negativity. Despair radicalizes the negativity of an inadequate or oppressive state of affairs, which is experienced in boredom, care, anxiety and melancholy, into a deficient mode of being as such. Despair reveals the failure of a human life as a whole. As a form of what should simply not be the case, despair reveals something about its unrealized opposite – successfully 'being-a-self'. This is why the range of phenomena associated with despair can serve as Kierkegaard's raw material, enabling him to start his analysis guided by the notion of a sickness of the self, even before he has attained a normative conception of the self.

After this methodological clarification, Theunissen approaches the phenomenon of despair with a transcendental question: 'How is the human being constituted, and how is his self to be conceived, if we are to make sense of the despair which he experiences as the reality of the self?'[21] This question immediately implies a second question: how is selfhood possible, given that it has to be presupposed in the process of liberation from the ever-present pull of despair? What makes selfhood possible as the process of the 'constant annihilation of the possibility of despair'? The answer, according to Kierkegaard, is that the being-a-self of the self can only succeed when, in its self-positing, it relates itself to another through whom it was itself posited. Human beings can only escape despair when the self is grounded 'transparently in the power which has posited it'. This thesis is justified with reference to the existential dialectic of two basic forms of despair. In our despondent not-wanting-to-be-ourselves, we experience the fact that we cannot get free of ourselves, that we are condemned to freedom and must posit ourselves. But in the subsequent stage of desperately wanting-to-be-ourselves, we experience the uselessness of our determined efforts to posit ourselves through our own power alone. We can only finally escape the despair of this *defiant* self-grounding when we become aware of the finitude of our freedom, and thereby of our dependence on an infinite power: 'The preconditions of not being in despair are also the preconditions of successfully being a self. The fact that human beings, in positing themselves, must accept the priority of the Other who has established them as self-positing, is thus the very definition of being a self.'[22]

(3) Theunissen regards this existential-dialectical demonstration of the grounding of being-a-self in faith as 'an argument which is difficult to controvert'. But even on his own account this argument requires a supplement which highlights the communicative structure of the capacity to be a self. Up till now, the explication of the fundamental structure of being-with-oneself-in-the-other has stated no more than the following: a human being, with her finite freedom, can only be herself when she frees herself from a narcissistically enclosed selfhood through recognition of the absolute freedom of God, and returns to herself from the infinite distance of a communication through faith with the sheerly Other. This explanation remains inadequate with regard to that trivial, innerworldly aspect of being-with-oneself-in-the-other which nonetheless offers us our primary encounter with communicative freedom. Theunissen criticizes the peculiar worldlessness of selfhood, which Kierkegaard emphasized in his negative treatment of despair. 'Of course, like Hegel, Kierkegaard understands selfhood as being-with-oneself-in-the-other, but on his account the other is found exclusively in God, and no longer in the world.'[23] The mere *reflexivity* of relating oneself to one's relation-to-self must be incorporated into the *intersubjectivity* of a surrender to the other: 'In love, we experience a spontaneous opening up of that primordial dimension of human freedom which faith has also revealed itself to be.'[24]

Thus Theunissen returns from a reconstructed Kierkegaard to a Hegel construed from the standpoint of a theory of communication. He grounds the complementary relation of love and communicative freedom in the absolute freedom and love of God. For 'all genuine love for other human beings . . . [is] . . . love of God'.

IV

Even if we go along with this extension of the existential-dialectical approach towards a theory of communication, a question still remains. It is not obvious that the Kierkegaardian argument which Theunissen so carefully reconstructs, and which must bear the real burden of proof, can deliver what it is supposed to deliver. The argument is supposed to show that, in order to be fully herself, a human being must assume that an empowerment through the absolute freedom of God has preceded her own communicative freedom. My reservations concern both the negativistic procedure, and the transfer of transcendental questions into the domain of anthropological facts.[25]

Naturally, we prefer not to be in despair. But our rejection of the negatively valued phenomenon of despair does not provide us with any positive distinguishing feature of the mere absence of the phenomenon – in other words, of not being in despair. This state may be a necessary condition of authentic selfhood, but it is not in itself a sufficient one. The *overcoming* of despair can only indicate a *successful* achievement of authentic selfhood if, *right from the beginning*, we establish a strong internal link between the phenomenon of despair and the mode of wanting-to-be-a-self. Furthermore, this has to be done through the use of clinical concepts such as psychic health. But then it is the normatively laden hermeneutic pre-understanding which discloses despair as a symptom of sickness. An interpretation which takes this approach can no longer be characterized as purely negativistic.

Moreover, the transcendental question of the conditions of selfhood could only be applied to an existential mood such as despairingly wanting-to-be-oneself, if the universality and irreplaceability of this 'fundamental state of mind' could be assumed. The analysis of transcendental conditions is only meaningful with regard to activities of a general nature, for which there are no functional equivalents. The transcendentalization of facts or existential experiences of the self has the unfortunate consequence of requiring us to attribute a world-constituting status to something which occurs within the world. If the transcendental grounding of selfhood as not-being-in-despair is to succeed, then a despondent wanting-to-be-oneself must belong to the human condition, and represent something like a general anthropological fact. We must also be able to rule out the possibility that different phenomena of a non-despondent wanting-to-be-oneself might appear as candidates for an analogous grounding of selfhood.

But there is a further issue. The real difficulty arises from the fact that what is to be explained, the point of departure for the question concerning conditions of possibility, must somehow already be a proven result. Transcendental questions are posed with reference to *substantiated* results, which fulfil corresponding conditions of valid-ity: true statements, grammatical sentences, binding speech acts, illu-minating theories, successful works of art and literature, and so on. From Theunissen's perspective, Kierkegaard, too, is inquiring into the conditions of possibility – if not of an achieved result – then of the process of successfully becoming a self. How is selfhood possible as the process of coming to terms with a despair which arises again and again? But in the case of Kant's question concerning the possibility of objective experience, it is a matter of rendering transparent the genesis of an accomplishment which is already accepted as valid, whose outcome we *encounter* as a fact in need of explanation, and which we can reproduce in as many examples as we like. But Kierkegaard starts from a very different kind of fact – from a despon-dent *wanting*-to-be-oneself which leaves open the question of success. What Kierkegaard wants to make transparent in its genesis has still not been validated. For the normal state is sickness, and only this provides the backdrop against which a 'healthy' kind of human existence can be delineated. The mode of successfully being a self can only be employed in a *hypothetical* way in the transcendental clarification of its conditions of possibility. Under these premises, faith could only be justified in functional terms, as the appropriate means of achieving the implied goal of wanting-to-be-oneself. But a functional argument is not sufficient to support the thesis which Theunissen wants to ground by means of Kierkegaard's argument, namely that: 'The emergence, out of freedom *from* oneself, of freedom *towards* oneself occurs at the deepest level of faith, as the commu-nicative genesis of selfhood.'[26] A faith which is functionally grounded destroys itself.

Theunissen overestimates the scope of the argument which he reconstructs from Kierkegaard. Even when he has recourse to the horizontal axis of interpersonal relations to supplement vertical communication with God, this does not bring the benefit he expects. It is true that the standpoint of formal-pragmatic analysis also regards those involved in communicative action as called on to achieve a transcendence from within, since, with every successful act of communication, they must orient themselves towards transcending validity-claims. But this modest truth is not enough for Theunissen. He would like to interpret successful acts of understanding in terms of a transcendence irrupting into history, the promissory presence of an absolute power which first makes our finite freedom possible. He repeatedly devises new arguments aimed at transforming Kierkegaard's 'leap of faith' into a transition which can be rationally thought through.[27] For Theunissen is too much of a philosopher to accept the statement which Dostoyevsky made (in a letter to Natalya Vonwisin dated 20 February 1854): 'If someone could prove to me that Christ is outside the truth, and if the truth really did exclude Christ, then I should prefer to stay with Christ and not truth.' Theunissen believes he has *philosophical reasons* capable of justifying and strengthening his commitment to a de-Hellenized *eschaton*. I am unable to accept these reasons, though I do accept that there can be rational motives for the conviction that one has such reasons.

V

One motive for such confidence can be found in the harsh polemic which Theunissen directs against the formalism of ethical thinking based on the moral 'ought'.[28] In this he follows Hegel's critique of Kant. Freedom in the moral sense of self-determination is manifested in the free will; and Kant terms the will 'free' when it lets itself be bound by moral insights and does what is in the equal interest of all. The task of moral theory is to clarify how correct moral judgements are possible. Basically, it is we who entrust ourselves with the rational resolution of practical questions. Since the ideas of justice and solidarity are inherently woven into communicative forms of socialization, discourse ethics seeks to clarify this fact in terms of the general pragmatic presuppositions of communicative action and argumentation. Theunissen renews Hegel's criticism of the impotence of this weak conception of morality. In reality, moral insights must secure the collaboration of concrete life forms, if they are to be practically effective.[29] For they can only appeal to the capacities of human beings who *need encouragement*, and who realize that, for all their dependence on favourable circumstances, they must ultimately rely on themselves.

The situation is different in the case of freedom in the ethical sense of self-realization. This is manifested in a conscious conduct of life, whose success cannot be attributed to the autonomy of finite beings alone. Theunissen seems to assume that ethics should explain the successful achievement of selfhood in the same way that moral theory explains how we have always already entrusted ourselves with making correct moral judgements. But in this case, 'ethics' would have to name a source of authority which could guarantee the possibility of an unspoiled life for everyone. For only thus could we assume the *capacity* to be a self as a transcendental fact, comparable to the ability to make correct moral judgements. But an unspoiled life does not lie within our power in the same way as correct moral judgement and action. Hence, when a similar transcendental question concerning conditions of possibility is posed with respect to successfully achieved selfhood, the fact that such selfhood is not entirely at our command requires it to be guaranteed by another power. This problematic issue makes clear why, even disregarding other considerations, Theunissen's argumentative strategy prevents him from renouncing the relation to an absolute freedom. But Kant realized that the logic of *this* kind of inquiry allows us to justify God as a practical postulate, at best. Our need to avoid falling into despair, and to hold open the prospect of happiness even under the domination of time, does not provide sufficient grounds for philosophy to announce a *dependable* outcome.

These considerations at least make the disputed point clear. Under the conditions of postmetaphysical thinking, can we answer the question of the good life – in modern guise, the question of successfully achieved selfhood – in a more than simply formal way? For example, can we provide a philosophical adumbration of the gospel message?

I discern a further motive for Theunissen's positive answer to this question in his selective description of communication. For the philosophy of dialogue simply exchanges the subject–object relation – the relation between first and third person which is privileged by the philosophy of consciousness – for the relation between first and second person. It does not exhaust the full meaning of the system of personal pronouns. The epistemic self-relation was initially envisaged as a form of self-observation. This reflection model comes to be replaced by a communicatively mediated self-relation which is structured in terms of the connection between I and Thou. It is conceived as a practical self-relation, as love or as communicatively mediated freedom, depending on whether the second or the first person is emphasized (in other words, as being-with-oneself-*in-the-other*, or being-*with-oneself*-in-the-other). But this approach elevates a special case, reciprocal ethical self-understanding concerning who one is and would like to be, to the status of the prototype of processes of reaching agreement in general. Indeed, the philosophy of dialogue directs attention away from the structure of the process of reaching agreement as such, and displaces it onto the existential experience of self achieved by the participants, an experience which is *brought about* by successful communication. For the sake of pure intersubjectivity, it overlooks the relation to the objective world built into the structure of reaching-agreement-concerning-something. It neglects what communication is *about*. As a result, the dimension of the validity of truth-claims is closed off in favour of the dimension of authenticity. And even this dimension can only be held open against the narcissistic pull of a worldless discourse of self-exploration by recourse to a universal which is introduced through the back door, as it were, and which is said to make communication possible in the first place.

This is why, as long ago as 1969, Theunissen made a plea for an 'absolute objectivity, which reaches beyond intersubjectivity and is the subject's ultimate ground'.[30] In a later study, devoted to the 'obscure' relation of universality and intersubjectivity, he repeats the thesis that 'in our self-realization, we have to achieve universality'.[31] Theunissen believes he cannot afford to give up the fundamentalistic connection to an authority which guarantees objectivity and truth, because otherwise 'intersubjectivity . . . is only an extension of subjectivity'.[32] But such a corrective ceases to be necessary if we free the structure of reaching-an-agreement-concerning-something from its restriction to the 'other'. This is a restriction which typifies the philosophy of dialogue. If we *integrate* the stance towards something in the objective world with the performative attitudes of the first- and second-person participants, then the complementarity of communicative freedom and love affirmed by Theunissen also disintegrates. Communicative freedom then takes on the profane, but by no means contemptible form of the responsibility of communicatively acting subjects. It consists in the fact that participants can orient themselves towards questions of validity. They do this when they raise validity-claims, when they take positive or negative stances towards the valid-ity-claims of others, and when they accept illocutionary obligations.

The interplay of finite subjects' communicative freedom opens an horizon which *also* enables us to experience the domination of the past over the future as a mark of the wounded history of both soci-eties and persons. Whether we adapt cynically to this reality, submit to it with melancholy, or despair over it and over ourselves, is revealed by those phenomena in which Theunissen rightly takes such an intense interest. But the philosopher will give a *different* description of these phenomena from the theologian, even though it need by no means be a discouraging one. Reflections from damaged life are equally the concern of both; but once theological and philosophical discourses have become disentangled,[33] such reflections are distin-guished in terms of their status and their claims, Philosophical dis-courses can be recognized by the fact that they stop short of the rhetoric of fate and promised salvation.

Of course, if anomalies become the norm, which is something Theunissen takes for granted has occurred, then the phenomena begin to get blurred. In this case, to discern the relevant phenomena at all, it may be appropriate to do philosophy in the mode – but only *in the mode* – of negative theology.

Translated by Peter Dews

Notes

1   On Heidegger, see M. Theunissen, *Negative Theologie der Zeit* (Frankfurt am Main: Suhrkamp, 1991), pp. 343ff. On Horkheimer, see Theunissen, 'Society and History: A Critique of Critical Theory', in P. Dews, ed., *Habermas: A Critical Reader* (Blackwell: Oxford, 1999), pp. 241–71.

2   Michael Theunissen, *The Other: Studies in the Social Ontology of Husserl, Heidegger, Sartre and Buber* (Cambridge, Mass.: MIT Press 1984), p. 383 (trans. altered by Peter Dews).

3   See J. B. Metz, 'Anamnestic Reason', in A. Honneth et al., eds, *Cultural-Political Interventions in the Unfinished Project of Enlightenment* (Cam-bridge, Mass. and London: MIT Press, 1992), pp. 189–94.

4   *Negative Theologie der Zeit*, p. 370.

5   Ibid., pp. 370ff.

6   Cf. Jürgen Habermas, *The Past as Future*, tr. Max Pensky (Lincoln: University of Nebraska Press).

7   *Negative Theologie der Zeit*, p. 65.

8   Theunissen, 'Möglichkeiten des Philosophierens heute', in ibid., pp. 13–36.

9   Theunissen, *Sein und Schein* (Frankfurt am Main: Suhrkamp, 1978), p. 28.

10   Ibid., pp. 468ff.

11   Ibid., pp. 455ff.

12   Ibid., pp. 70ff, 88ff.

13   Ibid., p. 463.

14   Ibid., pp. 326ff.

15   This explains Theunissen's interest in the broader theme of the forgetfulness of time in metaphysical thought. In this context, Theunissen is concerned to develop an adequate concept of the futuristic presence of the 'time of eternity'. See Theunissen, 'Zeit des Lebens', in *Negative Theologie der Zeit*, pp. 299–320; also Theunissen, 'Metaphysics' Forgetfulness of Time: On the Controversy over Parmenides Frag. 8,5', in A. Honneth et al., eds, *Philosophical Interventions in the Unfinished Project of Enlightenment* (Cambridge, Mass. and London: MIT Press, 1992), pp. 3–28.

16   J. Habermas, 'Handlungen, Sprechakte, sprachlich vermittelte Interaktion und Lebenswelt', in *Nachmetaphysiches Denken* (Frankfurt am Main: Suhrkamp, 1988), pp. 63ff.

17   M. Theunissen, 'Zwangszusammenhang und Kommunikation', in *Kritische Gesellschaftstheorie* (Berlin: de Gruyter, 1981), pp. 41ff, and esp. pp. 53ff.

18   M. Theunissen, 'Negativität bei Adorno', in L. v. Friedeburg, J. Habermas, eds, *Adorno-Konferenz 1983* (Frankfurt am Main, 1983), pp. 41ff. My bracketed interpolations.

19   Cf. most recently the interesting work by G. Lohmann, *Indifferenz und Gesellschaft* (Frankfurt am Main: Suhrkamp, 1991).

20   M. Theunissen, *Das Selbst auf dem Grund der Verzweiflung* (Frankfurt am Main: Suhrkamp, 1991); cf. also the Introduction and Theunissen's contribution to M. Theunissen and W. Greve, eds, *Materialien zur Philosophie Sören Kierkegaards* (Frankfurt am Main: Suhrkamp, 1979).

21   *Das Selbst auf dem Grund der Verzweiflung*, p. 25.

22   *Negative Theologie der Zeit*, p. 354. In this treatise on Jesus' conception of prayer Theunissen summarizes the reconstruction of Kierkegaard's argument which he has developed elsewhere: pp. 345ff.

23   Ibid., p. 359.

24   Ibid., p. 360.

25   I thank Lutz Wingert for his critical comments.

26   *Negative Theologie der Zeit*, p. 360.

27   To this context belong Theunissen's interesting studies of the way in which psychiatric patients experience time: 'Können wir in der Zeit glücklich sein?' and 'Melancholisches Leiden unter der herrschaft der Zeit', in ibid., pp. 37–88 and 218–84. I read these attempts at a philosophical appropriation of the observations of psychologists (above all, in the school of Binswanger) as steps along the second of the three viable paths of philosophical thought which Theunissen has outlined.

28   *Negative Theologie der Zeit*, pp. 29–32.

29   J. Habermas, 'Was macht eine Lebensform "rational"?', in *Erläuterungen zur Diskursethik* (Frankfurt am Main, 1991), pp. 31–48.

30   'Society and History', p. 258.

31   M. Theunissen, *Selbstverwirklichung und Allgemeinheit* (Berlin: de Gruyter, 1982), p. 8.

32   'Society and History', p. 258; *Selbstverwirklichung und Allgemeinheit*, p. 27.

33   J. Habermas, 'Transcendence from Within, Transcendence in this World', in this volume, pp. 67–94.

6

Israel or Athens: Where does Anamnestic Reason Belong?

Johannes Baptist Metz on Unity amidst Multicultural Plurality

The thought of Johannes Baptist Metz fascinates me – not least because I recognize common purposes at work, albeit across a certain distance. The fact that similar problems should arise both for the theologian and for someone who adopts the philosophical position of methodological atheism is less surprising than the parallels between the answers. I would like to offer thanks to my theological contemporary by seeking to clarify the nature of these parallels.

Metz once used his own life history to illustrate that simultaneity of the non-contemporaneous which confronts us in today's multicultural, differentiated and decentred world society:

> I come from an arch-Catholic small town in Bavaria. To come from such a place is to come from a long way away. It is as though one had been born not some fifty (or sixty-five) years ago, but rather somewhere on the twilit margins of the middle ages. I was forced to learn painfully what others, what 'society', had apparently discovered long ago . . . : for example, democracy as an everyday political fact, coping with a diffuse public realm, rules for the handling of conflict, even in family life, and so on. There was much that seemed strange, and which I still find disturbing.[1]

Against this backdrop, Metz has always fought against a merely defensive attitude of the Catholic Church to modernity, and advocated a productive participation in the processes of the bourgeois and

post-bourgeois Enlightenment. If the biblical vision of salvation does
not mean simply liberation from individual guilt, but also implies collective liberation from situations of misery and oppression (and thus
contains a political as well as a mystical element), then the eschatological drive to save those who suffer unjustly connects up with those
impulses towards freedom which have characterized modern European history.

But, of course, a blindness towards the dialectical character of
enlightenment is just as fateful as an insensitivity towards the eman-
cipatory potential of this history. The Enlightenment remained igno-
rant of the barbaric reverse side of its own mirror for too long. Its
universal claims made it easy to overlook the particularistic kernel of
its European origin. This immobilized, rigidified rationalism has been
transformed into the stifling power of a capitalistic world civilization,
which assimilates alien cultures and abandons its own traditions to
oblivion. Christianity, which thought it could use this civilization as
an 'innocent catalyst for the worldwide transmission of its message
of hope', the Church which believed it could send out its missionaries in the wake of the European colonizers, participated unwittingly
in this dialectic of disenchantment and loss of memory. This explains
the diagnosis which Metz puts forward as a theologian, and the practical demand with which he confronts his Church.

The diagnosis runs as follows: A philosophical conception of
reason derived from Greece has so alienated a Hellenized Christianity from its own origins in the spirit of Israel that theology has
become insensitive to the outcry of suffering and the demand for universal justice (1 and 2). The demand can be formulated thus: A eurocentric Church, which sprang up on the ground of Hellenism, must
transcend its monocultural self-conception and, remembering its
Jewish origins, unfold into a culturally polycentric global Church.

(1) *Israel versus Athens.* Metz is tireless in defending the heritage
of Israel in Christianity. 'Jesus was not a Christian, but a Jew' – with
this provocative statement Metz not only opposes Christian anti-
Semitism, he not only confronts the *ecclesia triumphans* with its
deeply problematic posture as victor in the face of a blinded and
humiliated synagogue;[2] above all, he rebels against the apathy of a
theology which was seemingly untouched by Auschwitz.[3] This
critique has an existential-practical thrust. But it also implies that, in
pushing aside its Jewish origins, a Hellenized Christianity has cut
itself off from the sources of anamnestic reason. It has itself become

one expression of an idealistic form of reason, unburdened by fate and incapable of recollection and historical remembrance. Those who regard Christianity from an 'Augustinian' perspective as a synthesis of intellect and belief, one in which the intellect comes from Athens and the belief from Israel, 'halve' the spirit of Christianity.[4] In opposition to this division of labour between philosophical reason and religious belief, Metz insists on the rational content of the tradition of Israel; he regards the force of historical remembrance as an element of reason: 'This anamnestic reason resists the forgetting, and also the forgetting of forgetting, which lies concealed in every pure historicization of the past.'[5] From this standpoint the philosophy whose roots lie in Greece appears as the guardian of *ratio*, of the powers of understanding which only become reason through their fusion with the *memoria* which dates back to Moses and his prophetic revelation. This is why a theology which returns from its Hellenistic alienation to retrieve its own origins can claim the last word against philosophy: 'it returns to the indissoluble connection between *ratio* and *memoria* (in late modern terms: the grounding of communicative reason in anamnestic reason)'.[6]

When one considers this claim from a philosophical standpoint, it is not just the grounding role of anamnestic reason which appears contestable. The picture of the philosophical tradition is flattened out too. For this tradition cannot be subsumed under the category of Platonism. In the course of its history it has absorbed essential elements of the Judaeo-Christian heritage, it has been shaken to its very roots by the legacy of Israel. Admittedly, from Augustine via Thomas to Hegel, philosophical idealism has produced syntheses which transform the God whom Job encountered into a philosophical concept of God. But the history of philosophy is not just the history of Platonism, but also of the protests against it. These protests have been raised under the sign of nominalism and empiricism, of individualism and existentialism, of negativism or historical materialism. They can be understood as so many attempts to bring the semantic potential of the notion of a history of salvation back into the universe of grounding speech. In this way practical intuitions which are fundamentally alien to ontological thought and its epistemological and linguistic transformations have penetrated into philosophy.

Metz brings these non-Greek motifs together in the *single* focus of remembrance. He understands the force of recollection in Freud's sense as the analytical force of making conscious, but above all in

Benjamin's sense as the mystical force of a retroactive reconciliation. Remembrance preserves from decay things we regard as indispensable, and yet which are now in extreme danger. This religious conception of 'salvation' certainly transcends the horizon of what philosophy can make plausible under the conditions of postmetaphysical thinking. But the concept of a saving remembrance paves the way for the disclosure of a domain of religious motives and experiences which long stood clamouring at the gates of philosophical idealism, before they were finally taken seriously, and disrupted from within a reason oriented towards the cosmos. But disruption was not the end of the story. The Greek logos has transformed itself on its path from the intellectual contemplation of the cosmos, via the self-reflection of the knowing subject, to a linguistically embodied reason. It is no longer fixated on our cognitive dealings with the world – on being as being, on the knowing of knowing, or the meaning of propositions which can be true or false. Rather the idea of a covenant which promises justice to the people of God, and to everyone who belongs to this people, a justice which extends through and beyond a history of suffering, has been taken up in the idea of a community tied by a special bond. The thought of such a community, which would entwine freedom and solidarity within the horizon of an undamaged intersubjectivity, has unfolded its explosive force even within philosophy. Argumentative reason has become receptive to the practical experiences of threatened identity suffered by those who exist historically.

Without this subversion of Greek metaphysics by notions of authentically Jewish and Christian origin, we could not have developed that network of specifically modern notions which come together in the thought of a reason which is both communicative and historically situated. I am referring to the concept of subjective freedom and the demand for equal respect for all – and specifically for the stranger in her distinctiveness and otherness. I am referring to the concept of autonomy, of a self-binding of the will based on moral insight, which depends on relations of mutual recognition. I am referring to the concept of socialized subjects, who are individuated by their life histories, and are simultaneously irreplaceable individuals and members of a community; such subjects can only lead a life which is genuinely their own through sharing in a common life with others. I am referring to the concept of liberation – both as an emancipation from degrading conditions and as the utopian project of a harmonious form of life. Finally, the irruption of historical thought into philosophy has fostered insight into the limited span of human life. It has made us more aware of the narrative structure of the histories in which we are caught up, and the fateful character of the events which confront us. This awareness includes a sense of the fallibility of the human mind, and of the contingent conditions under which even our unconditional claims are raised.

The tension between the spirit of Athens and the legacy of Israel has been worked through with no less an impact in philosophy than in theology. Philosophical thought is not exhausted by the synthetic labours of idealism, an idealism which the ecclesiastically structured, pagan Christianity of the West theologized. And this means that the critique of Hellenized Christianity does not automatically apply to argumentative reason, to the impersonal reason of the philosophers as such. Anamnesis and story-telling can also provide reasons, and so drive philosophical discourse forward, even though they cannot be decisive for it. Although profane reason must remain sceptical about the mystical causality of a recollection inspired by the history of salvation, although it cannot simply accept a general promise of restitution, philosophers need not leave what Metz calls 'anamnestic reason' entirely to the theologians. This I would like to show with reference to two themes which are of particular concern to Metz, one from the perspective of theology, and the other from that of Church politics.

(2) *The Problem of Theodicy.* The question of the salvation of those who have suffered unjustly is perhaps the most powerful moving force behind our continuing talk of God. Metz is decisively opposed to any Platonized softening of this question, which confronts Christians after Auschwitz more radically than ever.[7] In this case too, it was the conceptual tools of the Greek tradition which made it possible to separate the God of salvation from the Creator God of the Old Testament, freeing Him of responsibility for the barbarity of a sinful humankind. God Himself was not to be drawn into His creation, shot through, as it is, with suffering. Against this idealistic dilution of suffering, Metz invokes a 'culture of loss', a culture of remembrance which could keep open, without false consolation, the existential restlessness of a passionate questioning of God. An eschatologically driven anticipation, a sensitivity towards a suspended future, one which nevertheless already reaches into the present, would thereby be encouraged.[8] The biblical anticipation of the future

must not, in line with Nietzsche's doctrine of the Eternal Return, be
absorbed into a Greek understanding of eternity.[9]

But even this protest, which reaches inward towards the innermost
domains of religious experience, finds a parallel in those counter-
traditions of philosophical thought which have insisted on the positivity and obstinacy of the negative, as opposed to the Neo-Platonic
conception of descending gradations of the good and the true. In a
similar way to theologies which culminate in eschatology, this tradition, which stretches from Jakob Böhme and Franz Baader, via
Schelling and Hegel, to Bloch and Adorno, transforms the experience
of the negativity of the present into the driving force of dialectical
reflection. Such reflection is intended to break the power of the past
over what is to come. Since philosophy does not begin from the
premise of an almighty and just deity, it cannot make use of the question of theodicy in its plea for a culture of loss – for a sense of what
has failed and been withheld. But in any case, philosophy today is
less concerned with the idealistic transfiguration of a reality in need
of salvation than with indifference towards a world flattened out by
empiricism, and rendered normatively mute.

The fronts have been reversed. The historicism of paradigms and
world-pictures, now rife, is a second-level empiricism which undermines the serious task confronting a subject who takes up a positive
or negative stance towards validity-claims. Such claims are always
raised here and now, in a local context – but they also transcend all
merely provincial yardsticks. When one paradigm or world picture is
worth as much as the next, when different discourses encode everything that can be true or false, good or evil, in different ways, then
this closes down the normative dimension which enables us to identify the traits of an unhappy and distorted life. We can no longer recognize a life unworthy of human beings, and experience the loss this
involves. Philosophy, too, pits the force of anamnesis against a historicist forgetting of forgetting. But now it is argumentative reason
itself which reveals, in the deeper layers of its own pragmatic presuppositions, the conditions for laying claim to an unconditional
meaning. It thereby holds open the dimension of validity-claims
which transcend social space and historical time. In this way it makes
a breach in the normality of mundane events, which are devoid of
any promissory note. Without this, normality would close itself her-
metically against any experience of a solidarity and justice which is
lacking. However, such a philosophy, which takes up the thought of

community in the notion of a communicative, historically situated reason, cannot offer assurances. It stands under the sign of a transcendence from within, and has to content itself with the reasoned resolve of a sceptical but non-defeatist 'resistance to the idols and demons of a world which holds humanity in contempt'.

The relation between philosophy and theology shifts yet again in connection with the other theme, which crucially concerns Metz in the domain of Church politics and Church history. Here philosophy does not simply strive to appropriate semantic potentials which have been preserved in the religious tradition, as is the case with the question of theodicy. It can even assist a theology which aims to clarify the status of Christianity and the Church in the light of a pluralism of cultures and understandings of the world.[10]

(3) *The Polycentric World Church.* Since the second Vatican Council, the Church has been confronted with the double task of opening itself up from within to the multiplicity of cultures in which Catholic Christianity has established itself, and of seeking a bold dialogue with non-Christian religions, rather than lingering in defensive apologetics. The same problem occurs in both domains: how can the Christian Church retain its identity despite its cultural multivocity; and how can Christian doctrine maintain the authenticity of its search for truth in its discursive engagement with competing images of the world? A Church which reflects on the limitations of its eurocentric history, seeking to attune Christian doctrine to the hermeneutic departure points of non-Western cultures, cannot start from the 'idea of an ahistorical, culturally unbiased and ethnically innocent Christianity'. Rather, it must remain aware both of its theological origins and of its institutional entanglement with the history of European colonialism. And a Christianity which takes up a reflexive attitude to its own truth claims in the course of dialogue with other religions cannot rest content with an 'inconsequential or patronizing pluralism'. Rather, it must hold fast to the universal validity of its promise of salvation, whilst avoiding all assimilationist tendencies and entirely renouncing the use of force.[11]

From this perspective, the polycentric Church even seems to offer a model for dealing with the political problem of multiculturalism. In its internal relations it appears to provide the pattern for a democratic constitutional state, which allows the different life-forms of a multicultural society the right to flourish. And in its external relations such a Church could be a model for a community of nations which regulates its relations on the basis of mutual recognition. But, on closer inspection, it becomes clear that things are in fact the other way round. The idea of the polycentric Church depends in turn on insights of the European Enlightenment and its political philosophy.

Metz himself affirms the legacy of a rational conception of law which has been hermeneutically sensitized to its eurocentric limitations: Europe is

> the cultural and political home of a universalism whose kernel is strictly anti-eurocentric ... Admittedly, the universalism of the Enlightenment, which sought freedom and justice, was at first only semantically universal, and in its concrete application it has remained particularistic right up to the present day. But this universalism has also founded a new political and hermeneutic culture, one which aims at the recognition of the dignity of all human beings as free subjects. The recognition of cultural otherness must not abandon this universalism of human rights, which has been developed in the European tradition. It is this universalism which ensures that cultural pluralism does not simply collapse into a vague relativism, and that a supposed culture of sensitivity remains sensitive to issues of truth.[12]

However, Christianity cannot expect its ethically saturated conceptions of the history of salvation or of the created order to receive universal recognition *in the same sense* as a procedurally formulated theory of law and morality, which claims to ground human rights and the principles of the constitutional state with the help of a concept of procedural justice.[13] This is why even Metz understands the universality of the offer of salvation as an 'invitation' to all, which has to be practically tested, and not in terms of the claim to rational acceptability which has characterized the emergence of rational law, for example. Even the polycentric world Church remains *one* of several communities of interpretation, each of which articulates its own conception of salvation, its vision of an unspoiled life. These struggle with one another over the most convincing interpretations of justice, solidarity, and salvation from misery and humiliation. The Church must internalize this outsider perspective, make its own this gaze which is directed upon it. To achieve this it makes use of ideas which were developed by the European Enlightenment, ideas which, today, must be put into effect in democratically constituted multicultural societies, as well as in relations of recognition between the nations and cultures of this earth which are based on respect for human rights.

In multicultural societies basic rights and the principles of the constitutional state form the points of crystallization for a political culture which unites all citizens. This in turn is the basis for the coexistence of different groups and subcultures, each with its own origin and identity. The *uncoupling of these two levels of integration* is needed to prevent the majority culture from exercising a power of definition over the whole political culture. Indeed, the majority culture must subordinate itself to the political culture, and enter into a non-coercive exchange with the minority cultures. A similar situation obtains within the polycentric world Church. A shared Christian self-understanding must emerge within it, one which no longer coincides with the historically determining traditions of the West, but merely provides the backdrop which enables the Western tradition to become aware of its eurocentric limitations and peculiarities.

Another kind of hermeneutic self-reflection is required of Catholic Christianity as a whole in its relation to other religions. Here the analogy with a Western world which is coming to accept decentred and unprejudiced forms of exchange with non-Western cultures breaks down. For in this case we presuppose a common basis of human rights, which are presumed to enjoy a general and rationally motivated recognition. By contrast, in the case of the dialogical contest between religious and metaphysical world views, a common conception of the good which could play the same role as this shared legal and moral basis is lacking. This means that this contest has to be played out with a reflexive awareness that all concerned move in the same universe of discourse, and respect each other as collaborative participants in the search for ethical-existential truth. To make this possible a culture of recognition is required which takes its principles from the secularized world of moral and rational-legal universalism. In this domain, therefore, it is the philosophical spirit of political enlightenment which lends theology the concepts with which to make sense of moves towards a polycentric world Church. I say this without any intention of scoring points. For the political philosophy which performs this role is just as deeply marked by the thought of a community bound by covenant as it is by the idea of the polis. To this extent, it appeals to a biblical heritage. And it is this heritage to which Metz also appeals, when he reminds the contemporary Church that, in the name of its mission, it must 'seek freedom and justice for all', and be guided by 'a culture of the recognition of the other in his otherness'.[14]

Translated by Peter Dews

Notes

1   J. B. Metz, *Unterbrechungen* (Gütersloh: Güterloher Verlaghaus Mohn, 1980), p. 13.

2   K. J. Kuschel, ed., *Welches Christentum hat Zukunft? Dorothee Sölle und Johann Baptist Metz im Gespräch* (Stuttgart: Kreuz-Verlag, 1990), pp. 23ff.

3   J. B. Metz, *Jenseits bürgerlicher Religion* (Munich: Kaiser, 1980).

4   J. B. Metz, 'Anamnestic Reason', in Axel Honneth et al., eds, *Cultural-Political Interventions in the Unfinished Process of Enlightenment* (Cambridge, Mass. and London: MIT Press, 1992), pp. 189–94.

5   J. B. Metz, 'Die Rede von Gott angesichts der Leidensgeschichte der Welt', in *Stimmen der Zeit*, 5, 1992, p. 24.

6   Ibid.

7   J. B. Metz, 'Im Angesicht der Juden. Christliche Theologie nach Auschwitz', in *Concilium*, 20, 1984, pp. 382–9.

8   See 'Die Rede von Gott angesichts der Leidensgeschichte der Welt'. M. Theunissen speaks in this context of a 'proleptic future'. See 'Communicative Freedom and Negative Theology', pp. 110–28 in this volume.

9   M. Theunissen, *Negative Theologie der Zeit* (Frankfurt am Main: Suhrkamp, 1991), p. 368.

10 J. B. Metz, 'Theologie im Angesicht und vor dem Ende der Moderne', in *Concilium*, 20, 1984, pp. 14–18.

11 J. B. Metz, 'Im Aufbruch zu einer kulturell polyzentrischen Weltkirche', in F. X. Kaufmann, J. B. Metz, *Zukunftsfähigkeit* (Freiburg: Herder, 1987), pp. 93–115.

12 J. B. Metz, 'Perspektiven eines multikulturellen Christentums', MS, Dec. 1992.

13 John Rawls, *A Theory of Justice* (Cambridge, Mass.: Harvard University Press, 1971). J. Habermas, *Between Facts and Norms* (Cambridge: Polity, 1996).

14 Metz, *Zukunftsfähigkeit*, p. 118.

7

Tracing the Other of
History in History

Gershom Scholem's Sabbatai Ṣevi

Sixteen years after the publication of the English original, a German translation of Gershom Scholem's *The Main Currents of Jewish Mysticism* appeared in 1957. Those who regarded this book, when it came out in Germany, as the masterwork of a great scholar of the Kabbalah were soon obliged to revise their views. For in the same year Scholem published a large-scale biography of Sabbatai Ṣevi, who converted to Islam in 1666, the *kairos* of the heretical movement which he had launched. The work did not appear in English until 1973, in an expanded version authorized by Scholem. And almost two more decades were to elapse before the Jüdische Verlag published the long-planned German edition of this version. The book is 1093 pages in length; but this number would not satisfy Scholem's taste for kabbalistic number games. Once, while I was visiting him in Jerusalem, he presented me with an English copy of *Sabbatai Ṣevi*, and opened the last page with a meaningful look: it bore the round figure 1000. Perhaps he was thinking of the utopian features of those millenarian movements which – at the end of *our* millennium – are regarded with a good deal of scepticism. Of course, Scholem knew that page numbers are accidental. And yet, with his mischievous gesture, he wanted to leave open the question of whether this was *merely* chance.

The intentional ambiguity of this gesture is typical of the scholar's work as a whole. As a historian, he musters in his arsenal all the techniques of critical literary scholarship in order to search for a truth which is distorted, rather than disclosed, by the historical tradition. This applies not only to the truth about the Sabbatianic movement.

In general, Scholem regarded philological studies of the history of the Kabbalah as an ironic line of business:

> Does something of the inner law of what is fundamentally at issue remain visible to the philologist, or does what is essential disappear in this projection of the historical? The uncertainty of the answer to this question belongs to the nature of philosophical questioning as such; and so the hope which sustains this work is tinged with a certain irony.[1]

What hope is in question here? The reports of the mystics must have filled Scholem with the kind of expectation which, in earlier generations, was aroused by the words of the prophets. Scholem believed in the gift of mystical illumination. Admittedly, as he once told me, he had encountered such a capacity for inspiration only once in his life – in the person of his friend Walter Benjamin. In a dedication dating from 1941, Scholem characterized the genius of his friend by evoking 'the depth of the metaphysician, the penetration of the critic, and the knowledge of the scholar' – mystical gifts he did not mention. But his lifelong fixation with his friend, the passionate determination with which, right till the very end, he hunted down the scattered traces of the manuscript of the 'Arcades Project', a manuscript which was thought to be lost, suggest that Scholem saw Benjamin as a spirit haunted by illuminations.

But whatever is disclosed to the sight of the inward eye, the mystical vision, evades the word, the medium of tradition. The nature of mystical truth is paradoxical: 'It can be known, but not handed down, and the remains of it which can be handed down no longer contain it.'[2] Scholem searches history for the other of history. The unease which this paradox arouses is at the same time the driving force behind his work as a historian.

This unease also explains his interest in those heretical movements which seek through a praxis of intentional law-breaking to overcome evil once and for all and to accelerate the advent of the messianic age. Benjamin discovered antinomianism in an entirely different sphere – in contemporary surrealism, which aimed to release ambivalent feelings and renew primeval shocks through a calculated attack on ossified forms of perception. In these aesthetic experiments Scholem could see no more than a feeble imitation of those antinomian actions which had produced an incomparably greater force of renewal. Scholem, the bourgeois scholar, certainly did not identify with religious extremism. He reveals unsparingly the pathological traits and charlatanry of the ambivalent figure of Sabbatai Ṣevi. But he also emphasizes the innovative power of heretical movements. In terms of historically accessible documentation, they offer the most significant proof of the reality of a knowledge which, in its non-verbalizable core, eludes the historical tradition.

Sabbatianism is of course only the penultimate link in the chain of the Kabbalah's history, which Scholem has brought to light from obscure sources and corrupted manuscripts.

(1) He deals first of all with the doctrines of Isaak Luria, who founded a widely influential school in the middle of the sixteenth century, in Safed in Palestine. Lurian mysticism breaks in one primary respect with the dominant conceptions of the kabbalistic doctrine of the high Middle Ages, the Zohar. The neo-Platonic concepts of the Zohar could only define the evil and the untrue, and in general negative phenomena such as the harmful, the diseased and the hostile, in *privative* terms – as the obscuring or weakening of the Ideas, as matter sullying ideal being, so to speak. The negative lacked the spur of wilfulness, the character of the resistant, even the productive. For this reason, the problem of theodicy was defused right from the beginning. The question of how evil is possible at all in a world created by God can only be given a coherent formulation when we take the negative seriously in its distinctive positivity, and lead it back to its origin in the divine life-process itself.

This is what Luria's original idea of the *tsim-tsum* achieves. God, who in the beginning was everything, withdraws into Himself, implodes as it were, in order to make room for His creatures. Luria's image of the contraction or withdrawal into oneself is intended to explain the void out of which God then created heaven and earth. Through this initial contraction there arises (as Jakob Böhme will put it, in a curious convergence with Lurianic mysticism) a nature in God, a knot of wilfulness and egoity. The polar tension between this dark ground in God and His radiating love already determines the ideal process of creation, which occurs in God's body and thought. This culminates in the figure of the first Adam, Adam Kadmon. Or, more precisely, it would have so culminated, had a catastrophe not intervened. The vessels, which can no longer contain the sparks of divine light, break apart. As a result of this disruptive event, the rest of the process of creation acquires a new meaning: the lights which have been poured away and dispersed must be raised up again to their legitimate place of origin. The resurrection or restitution of the original order – the *tikkun* – would finally have reached its goal with the creation of the second, the earthly Adam, if the catastrophe had not repeated itself through the Fall. This time the process of creation slips out of the hands of God, so to speak. Now, for the first time, the creation emerges from the inner depths of God and continues in the external history of the world.

(2) The second link in the historical chain of reception of the Kabbalah is the echo which Lurianic mysticism finds amongst the Jewish people – in the century of the great emigrations after the Reconquista and the expulsion of the Jews from Spain. This event was shattering for the whole of Jewry. It lends a new relevance to the primordial biblical experience of exile. In the light of Lurianic mysticism the meaning of this exile for the history of salvation acquires a new interpretation. For it is seen as a repetition of the exile into which God had entered within Himself, prior to all creation. Luria himself presents the original contraction as a banishment which God must impose on Himself in order to set the process of creation in motion. But now this fraught drama of the becoming of God is transformed into a model of earthly history which promises salvation. For, since the Fall, part of the responsibility for the success of the resurrection of the fallen world has passed over to human beings themselves: 'The historical process and its innermost soul, the religious act of the Jew, prepare the way for the final restitution of all the scattered and exiled lights and sparks . . . Every act of man is related to this final task which God has set for His creatures . . . The redemption of Israel concludes the redemption of all things.'[3]

For Luria the appearance of the Messiah simply set the seal on the completion of a process of restoration sustained by the believers themselves. In the Jewish communities, which had been marked by the experience of exile and were threatened by further pogroms, the emphasis shifted. Rather than the power of prayer, it is the expectation of the Messiah which now moves into the foreground. An interest in the role and person of the Messiah which is alien to classic Lurianism develops.

(3) This is why the decisive link in the chain is provided by the doctrine of Nathan of Gaza. Even before his important meeting with Sabbatai Ṣevi, Nathan had visions which led him to interpret the role of the Messiah in a new way. The soul of the Messiah, which had already plunged into the abyss with the 'breaking of the vessels' is

held captive by the forces of evil. It is the holy serpent, who is encircled by the serpents of evil. The existence of the Messiah thus becomes profoundly ambivalent. In the last act of the world-historical drama of salvation the dialectic of intensifying darkness which had already occurred twice, in the breaking of the vessels, and in Adam's Fall, repeats itself for the third time. For the Messiah who has plunged into the abyss can finally subdue the ultimate and most obstinate forces of evil only with their own means. Nathan describes this struggle in the form of a commentary on the apocalypse: the Messiah will do astonishing and terrible things, and he will give himself up to martyrdom, in order to fulfil the will of his Creator.

In 1941 Scholem wrote in *Major Trends*:

> It is not my purpose here to present the swift rise and the sudden collapse of the Sabbatian movement in 1665 and 1666, from Sabbatai Ṣevi's proclamation of his Messianic mission to his renunciation of Judaism and adoption of Islam when he was led before the Turkish Sultan. I am not primarily concerned with the biography of the Messiah and his prophet, Nathan of Gaza, nor with the details of the tremendous religious mass movement which spread like wild-fire through the entire Diaspora – already prepared, as it were, for such an event by the new Kabbalism. Suffice it to say that very large numbers of people were swept on a tide of emotion and underwent the most extravagant forms of penance ... But hand in hand with penitence there also went boundless joy and enthusiasm, for at last there seemed to be visible proof that the sufferings of 1600 years had not been in vain. Before redemption had actually come it was felt by many to have become a reality. An emotional upheaval of immense force took place among the mass of the people.[4]

It is precisely this programme which Scholem then carries through with an immense effort of historical and philological erudition. The fact that, out of eight chapters in the book, he devotes less than one to Nathan of Gaza should not be allowed to deceive us as to who played the chief role. Nathan is the director of the play in which Sabbatai Ṣevi is a marionette.

Sabbatai requests a meeting with Nathan in the spring of 1665, in the first instance to seek peace for his soul. He comes to him as a patient to a psychiatrist. But it is Nathan who convinces him in the course of weeks of conversation that he is called to be the Messiah. And it is only the uncontested authority of the learned Nathan of

Gaza which can convince even the oldest friends and followers of Sabbatai Ṣevi of his identity as the Messiah:

> Nathan's character was very different from that of Sabbatai Ṣevi. We shall look in vain for any of the prophet's outstanding qualities in the Messiah: tireless activity, unwavering perseverance without manic-depressive ups and downs, originality of theological thought and considerable literary ability. Sabbatai's fumbling attempts in theology are pale shadows compared to the systematic audacity which made Nathan the first great theologian of heretical kabbalism. With all the charm, dignity and attractiveness of the 'man of sorrows . . . smitten of God and afflicted', Sabbatai lacked strength of character . . . Even in his moments of manic exaltation he did not really 'act', and the flurry of provocative gestures spent itself without producing permanent effects. At the height of the movement he remained passive, and his activity exhausted itself in increasingly bizarre and 'strange' acts. The two men complemented each other in a remarkable fashion, and without that combination the Sabbatian movement would never have developed. Sabbatai was a poor leader. Devoid of will power and without a programme of action, he was a victim of his illness and his illusion.[5]

(4) But if this is Scholem's view of the relation between these two principal figures, why was all his ambition invested in a biography of Sabbatai Ṣevi? Why did he commit himself, with a positivistic fervour worthy of the most prominent scholars of the German Historical School, to the detective work of unearthing the most trivial details of the life of this shady Messiah? And why did he then spend more than 1000 pages presenting them to us in the form of a brilliant historical novel drawing on original sources? In order to answer this question we must turn our attention to the last link in the chain – the reversal of heretical messianism into what Scholem terms 'religious nihilism'.

Scholem investigates this phenomenon using the example of the populist figure Jakob Frank, who appeared in Galicia as the reincarnation of Sabbatai Ṣevi, and in 1759 converted to Catholicism. Jakob Frank, too, pursued the path into the abyss as the subversive path to salvation: 'Abandon all laws and prescriptions, all virtues, modesty and chastity. Abandon holiness itself. Climb down into yourself as into a grave.'[6] Now it is not merely the bizarre actions of the Messiah which the antinomian doctrine of the holiness of sin explains. Rather, this doctrine is set up as the law of the law-violating praxis of the community as a whole.

What fascinates Scholem about this is the dialectical reversal of Messianism into enlightenment; for the utopian energies released by heretical messianism are directed by the French Revolution towards political goals in the here and now. The Frankist Moses Dobrushka follows this path in an exemplary way. He became a Catholic and, under the name of Thomas von Schönfeld, he became a spokesman for the Enlightenment policies of the Emperor Joseph, founded an order of Free Masons, and after the outbreak of the French Revolution, became a Jacobin in Strasbourg: 'In April 1794, aged forty, he mounted the scaffold with Danton – under the name Junius Frey.'[7] This reversal of religion into enlightenment illuminates the interesting connection between the history of the influence of the Kabbalah and Scholem's self-understanding as a scholar of the Kabbalah. Scholem is a historian who cannot step back behind the threshold of the historical Enlightenment, and yet wants no accommodation with the historicist 'smokescreen, which – in the form of the history of mystical traditions – conceals the space of the very thing itself'. For Scholem enlightenment is our fate, but this does not mean it should have the last word. He always regarded Marx and Freud as the real heretics; he is convinced that even the religious impulses of the last Sabbatians have not dissolved entirely into a political utopia. At the same time, we are all sons and daughters of the French Revolution. Scholem considered the reversal of religion into enlightenment as inevitable as it was unsatisfactory. And his own historical and philological research into the Kabbalah remained caught in this dichotomy.

Scholem had no other recourse than to incorporate the antinomian motive into his own practice; he buried himself in positivism, in order to penetrate through the smokescreen of historical facts from within. By turning outwards, in a resolutely scientist manner, towards the critical disclosure of the historical material, he sought to get nearer to a truth which transcends all history, since it is only revealed to the inner eye. I regard his obsessively detailed work on the biography of Sabbatai Ṣevi, a book which by all the standards of academic art is truly amazing, as being *also* a spiritual exercise – an exercise by means of which Scholem sought at least to *circle ever closer* to the visions of Nathan of Gaza. Only once, in his 'Ten unhistorical statements concerning the Kabbalah', did Scholem lift the visor of the scientific scholar, and reveal himself as a negative theologian. The third section deals with the mediated nature of the knowledge passed down to us through tradition and interpretation, knowledge which is repeatedly thwarted by the objectlessness of the highest knowing, since such knowing belongs to the domain of mystical inspiration. Scholem's train of reflection ends with a statement which could almost be regarded as comforting: ' "Who" is the last word of all theory, and it is quite astonishing that theory can go so far as to escape from the "What" to which its beginnings remain bound.'[8]

Translated by Peter Dews

Notes

1   G. Scholem, 'Zehn unhistorische Sätze über Kabbala', in *Judaica* 3 (Frankfurt am Main: Suhrkamp, 1973), p. 264.
2   Ibid., p. 264.
3   G. Scholem, *Major Trends in Jewish Mysticism* (New York: Schocken Books, 1961), p. 274.
4   Ibid., p. 288.
5   G. Scholem, *Sabbatai Ṣevi. The Mystical Messiah 1626–1676* (London: Routledge and Kegan Paul, 1973), pp. 207–8.
6   G. Scholem, 'Die Metamorphose des häretischen Messianismus', in *Judaica* 3, p. 208.
7   Ibid., p. 212.
8   Scholem, 'Zehn unhistorische Sätze über Kabbala', p. 266.

8

A Conversation About
God and the World

Interview with Eduardo Mendieta

Mendieta The slogan of the day is globalization, even if there is no consensus on what exactly it means. Some view it as a radically new political, economic, technological, social, and ecological order. Others contest the qualitative difference between globalization and other epochal markers like modernity, postmodernity, even postcoloniality. The latter see globalization as modernity raised to the second power, or modernity become self-reflexive. Curiously, however, the question of religion remains present but mute. To what extent do you see religion as being a precursor, a catalyst, even perhaps a "condition of possibility" of both modernity and globalization?

Habermas The themes of the Judaeo-Christian heritage help to explain the cultural, but not the social, modernization of the West. Through the reception of Greek philosophy (if one thinks of Toledo, for example), these impulses are also united with the impetus of Islam. We should also remember that for all three monotheistic religions it was above all the heretical movements and schisms that preserved a sensitivity for the more radical forms of revelation. From the sociological point of view, the modern forms of consciousness encompassing abstract right, modern science, and autonomous art (with the secularization and independence of the panel painting at its center) could never have developed apart from the organizational forms of Hellenized Christianity and the Roman Catholic Church, without the universities, monasteries, and cathedrals. This is especially true for the emergence of mental structures.

Unlike the range of early mythic narratives, the idea of God – that is, the idea of the unified, invisible God the Creator and Redeemer – signified a breakthrough to an entirely new perspective. With this idea, finite spirit acquired a standpoint that utterly transcends the this-worldly. But only with the transition to modernity does the knowing and morally judging subject appropriate the divine standpoint, insofar as it assumes two highly significant forms of idealization. On the one side, the subject objectifies external nature as the totality of states of affairs and events that are connected in a law-like manner. On the other, the subject expands the familiar social world into an unbounded community of all responsibly acting persons. In this way, the door is opened for reason to penetrate the opaque world in both dimensions – in the form of the cognitive rationalization of an objectified nature, and the social-cognitive rationalization of the totality of morally regulated interpersonal relationships.

My impression is that Buddhism is the only other world religion that achieved a comparable level of abstraction, and that, structurally regarded, carried out a similar conceptualization of the divine standpoint. Unlike the monotheistic world-views, Eastern religions are based not on the acting person but on the impersonal consciousness of an entirely indeterminate Something. They propel the dynamic of abstraction in the opposite direction: not via the heightening of personal achievements toward the "omnipotent," "omniscient," and "all-loving" God, but rather via the continuous negation of all possible properties of an object of perception and judgment. In this way, Buddhism draws near to the vanishing point of a pure or radical "Nothing" – to that which remains once we have abstracted from everything that makes any possible Something into a particular entity; to a not-Something, which Malewitsch's black squares attempt to express. The same cognitive operation which led the Greeks to the "Being of beings" in a theoretical intention, leads here, in a moral intention, to a "Nothing," which has shaken off everything constitutive of "something in the world."

But in fact, cultural and social modernization has not been completed in the regions dominated by Buddhism. In the West, Christianity not only fulfilled the cognitive initial conditions for modern *structures* of consciousness; it also demanded a range of *motivations* that were the great theme of the economic and ethical research of Max Weber. For the normative self-understanding of modernity, Christianity has functioned as more than just a precursor or a catalyst. Universalistic egalitarianism, from which sprang the ideals of freedom and a collective life in solidarity, the autonomous conduct of life and emancipation, the individual morality of conscience, human rights and democracy, is the direct legacy of the Judaic ethic of justice and the Christian ethic of love. This legacy, substantially unchanged, has been the object of a continual critical reappropriation and reinterpretation. Up to this very day there is no alternative to it. And in light of the current challenges of a postnational constellation, we must draw sustenance now, as in the past, from this substance. Everything else is idle postmodern talk.

Surely, the globalization of markets – the rise of electronically interconnected financial markets and the acceleration of capital mobility – have led to a transnational economic regime, markedly diminishing the leading industrialized nations' capacities for action. But the intensification and expansion of communication and commerce creates only a new infrastructure, and not a new orientation or a new form of consciousness. This new stage in the development of capitalism takes place *within* a horizon of social modernity that has remained essentially the same, and within the normative self-understanding developed in that horizon since the end of the eighteenth century. As I said, religion and the Church served an important role as pacemakers for this mentality. But the same cannot be said for the emergence of globalized commerce and communication. Christianity is far more deeply affected and challenged by the unforeseen consequences of this new infrastructure, as are other forms of "objective Spirit."

Mendieta The other half of the prior question would raise the issue of the relationship of both modernity and globalization to religion in the following way: to what extent must we think of contemporary forms of religion, and one should also add of theological reflection, as products of both modernity and globalization? Is there a sense in which contemporary forms of religion, as practices and social institutions, beliefs and forms of experience, are only understandable as products or processes of modernization?

Habermas The Christian churches must meet the challenges of globalization by appropriating their own normative potential more radically. The *Oecumene* is only now becoming ecumenical in a nonpaternalistic sense; only now is the Church becoming a polycentric world Church, a topic that has been the preoccupation of my friend Johannes Baptist Metz. The universalism of the world religions is only now emerging in a strongly interculturalist sense; the Christian ethic is broadening itself only today into a truly inclusive global ethics – a project that Hans Küng has pursued. But your question is aiming deeper than this. If I am correct, it refers to the transformation of religious consciousness which began in the West with the Reformation, and since then has spread to other world religions: the "modernization" of faith itself. This same modernization, for which both religion and the Church fulfilled important initial conditions, generated a secularized society which then, in turn, demanded a cognitive restructuring of the forms of religious faith and Church praxis.

Revealed religions are transmitted in the dogmatic form of "doctrine." But in the West, Christian doctrine developed through the conceptual medium and scholastic form of philosophy, in the form of a scientific [*wissenschaftlich*] theology. This internal rationalization allowed a cognitive change of form, which, despite Luther's own ambivalence, led to a reflexive mode of faith in the wake of the Reformation. In modern societies, religious doctrine has to accommodate itself to the unavoidable competition with other forms of faith, and other claims to truth. It no longer moves in a self-contained universe directed, so to speak, by its own absolute truth. Every religious doctrine today encounters the pluralism of different forms of religious truth – as well as the skepticism of a secular, scientific mode of knowing that owes its social authority to a confessed fallibility and a learning process based on long-term revision. Religious dogmas and the attitude of the faithful have to harmonize the illocutionary meaning of religious speech – the affirmation of the truth of a religious statement – with both facts. Each religious faith must build a relationship with competing messages of other religions, just as much as with the claims of science and a secularized, halfway-scientific common sense.

Thus modern faith becomes reflexive. Only through self-criticism can it stabilize the inclusive attitude that it assumes within a universe of discourse *delimited* by secular knowledge and *shared* with other religions. This decentered background consciousness of the relativity of one's own standpoint certainly does not necessarily lead to the relativization of articles of faith themselves, but it is nevertheless characteristic of the modern form of religious faith. Further, it is constitutive for what John Rawls calls the reasonableness of

"reasonable comprehensive doctrines." This has the important political consequence that the community of the faithful can ascertain
why it must refrain from the use of violence – and state-sponsored
violence above all – as a means for the promotion of religious belief.
In this sense, what we call the "modernization of faith" is an important cognitive presupposition for the achievement of religious toler-
ation and the construction of a neutral state power.

We call "fundamentalist" those religious movements which, given
the cognitive limits of *modern* life, nevertheless persist in practicing
or promoting a return to the exclusivity of premodern religious
attitudes. Fundamentalism lacks the epistemic innocence of those
long-ago realms in which the world religions first flourished, and
which could somehow still be experienced as limitless. Only contemporary China can provide some small taste of this consciousness
of imperial boundlessness, which once grounded the limited "universalism" of the world religions. But modern conditions are compatible only with a strict, Kantian form of universalism. This is why
fundamentalism is the false answer to an epistemological situation
which demands insight into the inevitability of religious tolerance
and imposes on the faithful the burden of having to endure the secularization of knowledge and the pluralism of world pictures regardless of the religious truths they hold.

Mendieta   Religion may be understood as a form of human communication, and as such it was always impacted by transformations
in the means and modes of communication. Today the information
and telecommunications revolutions are irreparably transforming
both the means and the modes of communication. Is it possible
that we may be witnessing the obsolescence of older forms of
human interaction, and the birth of new ones that might catalyze
the birth of new religions, new churches, new forms of piety and
prayer?

Habermas   I cannot say much on this point, since this is the kind of
question that really can only be answered "from within," from the
point of view of the participant. And sociologically speaking I have
not studied any of the new, de-institutionalized and de-differentiated
forms of religiosity. All the great world religions were familiar with
anti-clerical revival movements that criticized existing institutions, or
with mystical movements, or the subjectivism of highly emotional

forms of devotion, of which Pietism is an example for us. This same impulse survives today in different forms. In any event, what I see nowadays in the "esoterica" sections of bookshops appears to me more as a symptom of ego weakness and regression, the expression of a yearning for an impossible return to mythical forms of thought, magical practices, and closed worldviews, that the Church overcame in its battle against "the heathens." But history teaches us that religious sects can be very innovative. So maybe not everything on the market is Californian claptrap or neopaganism.

But in this matter a debate, perhaps the chance for a genuine discourse, seems to be lacking. Reading Aquinas' *Summa Contra Gentiles*, I am struck by the complexity, the sheer degree of differentiations, the gravity, and the stringency of a dialogically constructed argument. I am an admirer of Aquinas. He represents a form of spirit that is able to ground its authenticity from out of its own resources. It is also simply a fact that there is no longer this kind of firmament in the morass of contemporary religiosity. In a homogenizing media society, everything loses its gravity, perhaps even institutionalized Christianity itself.

Mendieta   In your work you sometimes refer to Europe's mission in relation to the world – to a "second chance" in history that a united Europe might promise. To what extent is that mission compromised, that is, rendered suspect, by its relationship to Christianity? In more pointed terms, if one reads carefully between the lines of most of the commentary written by the philosophers of the global state (like Fukuyama, Huntington, etc.) one will note that there is the assumption that globalization is the continuation of the Christian civilizing project, and that whatever stands in its way is "oriental" despotism, Muslim fundamentalism, etc. To this extent, globalization is counterposed against the non-West in a mission of redemption and salvation.

Habermas   Well, there can be no disputing that there is an unholy trinity of colonialism, Christianity, and Eurocentrism. The dark, obverse side of the mirror of modernization, which otherwise wants to reflect only the image of the spread of civilization, human rights, and democracy, has indeed been illuminated to some extent. But in the end, egalitarianism and universalism (which today's neoliberal apologists for an unfettered global commercial regime trumpet just as proudly as yesterday's colonial masters once did Christianity) *also* provide us with the only convincing criteria for criticizing the miserable state of our economically fragmented, stratified, and un-pacified global society. Who in the present could still want to justify the monstrously brutal process of global social modernization since the fifteenth century from a normative point of view? And yet, the current state of the world, "the modern condition," is without any clearly recognizable alternative, and is indeed nothing for which we in the present have to assume retrospective responsibility, or assign retrospective blame.

As the Pol Pot regime in Cambodia, the "Shining Path" in Peru, or the dictatorship of impoverishment in North Korea all illustrate, there is no reasonable exit-option left to us from a capitalist world society today, after the failed experiment of Soviet communism. Transformations of global capitalism, which could lead from a per-manent state of affairs to a self-accelerating "creative destruction," now seem only possible from within. This is why we need a form of self-referential politics, which would aim at strengthening capacities for political action itself, and at reigning in an uncontrolled economic dynamic both within and beyond what still counts as the authorita-tive level of nation-states. I have described this in my book *The Post-national Constellation*.[1] The fact that we can act only under the conditions of a form of societal modernity not of our own choosing obviously doesn't imply that we must act as missionaries of a Western culture that first created it.

Let's take the example of human rights. Notwithstanding their European origins, human rights now compose the universal language in which global commercial relationships come under normative regulation. In Asia, Africa, and South America, they also constitute the only language in which the opponents and victims of murderous regimes and civil wars can raise their voices against violence, repression, and persecution, against injuries to their human dignity. But to the extent that human rights are accepted as a transcultural language, disagreements over their appropriate interpretation between cultures have only intensified. Insofar as this intercultural discourse on human rights occurs under conditions of reciprocal recognition, it also has the potential of leading the West toward a decentered understanding of a normative construct that no longer remains the property of Europeans, and can no longer mirror the particularities of one culture.

Surely, the West still maintains a privileged access to the resources of power, wealth, and knowledge in our world. But it is in our own best interest that the project that proceeds from here of developing a just and peaceful global civilization not be discredited from the outset. Thus the West, molded by the Judaeo-Christian tradition, must reflect on one of its greatest cultural achievements: the capacity for decentering one's own perspectives, self-reflection, and a self-critical distancing from one's own traditions. The West must abstain from any non-discursive means, must be only one voice among many, in the hermeneutical conversation between cultures. In a word: overcoming Eurocentrism demands that the West make proper use of its own cognitive resources. This is, God knows, easier said than done, as the current example of the selective prosecutions and the problematic implementation of human rights policies in the former Yugoslavia illustrates. But that is a different topic.

Mendieta   Let me raise the stakes on this question. To what extent can we think of the West without Athens, Rome, or Jerusalem? Conversely, to what extent can we think of a postnational global order without the history of religious conflict and the ever-present possibility of its exacerbation?

Habermas   You correctly point out the internal tensions along the fault lines of Western culture. Jerusalem, Rome, Athens – this is the distinctive tension between monotheism, learning, and the republican tradition that the West has always had to bear, without reducing one to any of the others. As far as the relation between Athens and Jerusalem is concerned, the Hellenization of Christianity – theology as the scientization of the redemptive mission – always displayed a tendency to water down the essence of the Christian message. Job's question – the question of God's justice in the face of the experience of suffering, and of annihilation in godforsaken darkness – loses its radical nature within the horizon of Greek thought, as well as with the Church fathers. Where was God in Auschwitz? Along the axis of Rome and Jerusalem, we can see a similar loss of tension: on the one hand, the secularization and politicization of the biblical mission, and on the other side the political-theological expropriation of the rational core of a secularized politics. Finally, we Germans are also familiar with the cultural-religious haze of a pretentious if also depoliticized neo-humanism that sublimates the Roman-republican

beneath the Greek-spiritual, submerging the pragmatics of daily existence into the blurry aura of the extraordinary. Among us, Brecht –
and not Hannah Arendt – belongs to the very few party faithful of
"Rome," who still recognized the fatal consequences of German
classicism's fixation on Greek antiquity.

These symbiotic misdevelopments emerge when the contradictory
elements of a tense cultural synthesis lose their distinct individuality.
We see this in the relation between philosophy and religion as well:
the existential meaning of the individual soul's liberation through the
promise of salvation of God the Redeemer cannot be harmonized
with the contemplative elevation and the intuitive fusion of finite
spirit with the Absolute.

Things are much the same, on the global level, concerning the
tension between different cultures and the world religions. Individual cultures can only make a positive contribution to the rise of a
world culture if they are respected in their own, stubborn individuality. This tension needs to be *stabilized*, not resolved, if the net of
intercultural discourse is not to be torn.

Mendieta As we look over the philosophical achievements, rup-
tures, and continuities of the West, we see a perennial confrontation
with, but also connection to, the Judeo-Christian tradition. The
German philosophical version of this confrontation and connection
with the Judeo-Christian tradition is particularly noteworthy in its
obvious claim to both Athens and Rome, and Jerusalem with great
pains and reservations: from Jakob Böhme and Meister Eckhart, to
Martin Luther, Kant, Hegel, Marx, and more recently in this century Heidegger, Löwith, Bloch, Adorno, Horkheimer, and naturally
Benjamin. One may even say that Christendom survived in the great
philosophical mansions of German philosophy. And if that is the
case, then how can European philosophy open itself up to a global
order without at the same time having to challenge and reflect on its
religious inheritance? And if this is to be done, how?

Habermas Yes, I see the intense encounter with "strong" alternative
traditions as a chance to become more fully aware of one's own roots;
in this case our own rootedness in the Judaeo-Christian tradition. As
long as participants inhabit the same discursive universe, there is no
hermeneutic impulse to reflect on otherwise self-evident, unarticu-
lated background motivations. This spur to reflection doesn't prevent

intercultural understanding; indeed it is what makes it possible in the first place. And all participants must get clear on the particularity of their own respective mental presuppositions before the discursive presuppositions, interpretations, and value orientations they hold in common can come to light.

The West now encounters other cultures in the form of the overpowering scientific and technological infrastructure of a capitalist world civilization. Our own forms of rationality have materialized in it. We no longer confront other cultures as alien since their structures still remind us of previous phases of our own social development. What we *do* encounter as alien within other cultures is the stubborn distinctiveness of their religious cores. Alternative religions are, in our own eyes, the inspirational sources for other cultures. This explains not just the ongoing relevance of Max Weber, but also the challenge that European philosophy faces in posing just the question that you insist on here.

I would certainly want to draw sharper distinctions within the German tradition whose members you name. As opposed to English, French, or American philosophy, Germany has had relatively few politically minded intellectual figures. The Roman-republican heritage finds an expression only with Kant and Reinhold, Heine and Marx. On the other hand, the experience of the French Revolution inspired the Tübingen seminarians – Hegel, Schelling, and Hölderlin – to reconcile Athens and Jerusalem with each other, and to reconcile both of them with a modernity that essentially generates its own normative self-understanding from the egalitarian, universalistic spirit of the Jewish and Christian traditions. In the course of this project, Hegel's central concern was to set basic metaphysical concepts into dialectical motion within the medium of *Heilsgeschichte*, the history of salvation. Still, it's possible to distinguish within German philosophy all the way to the present between a rather aesthetic, Platonistic line and another current, oriented toward social philosophy and the philosophy of history.

The tradition that remains dedicated to the Greeks and to the projects of ontology and cosmology persists today not only in the classical form of philosophical idealism, as in Dieter Henrich's theory of self-consciousness. The metaphysical interest in the constitution of beings as such also persists in the language of formal semantics and epistemology. It can even be negotiated in the language of naturalism, as in contemporary work on mind–body relations. In its basic projects and concepts, this philosophical mainstream differs from those philosophical schools that were revolutionized by historical thought. These latter appropriated the existential or world-historical themes which had previously been reserved for theology and its reflections on a history of salvation. The exemplary figures here are, naturally, the great outsiders of the nineteenth century – Marx, Kierkegaard, and Nietzsche. Here also belong all those thinkers whose work offered a diagnosis of their own times, and whose work promoted categories of lived historical experience into basic philosophical concepts. I am thinking of concepts like sociality, language, praxis, embodiment, contingency, action, historical time, intersubjective understanding, individuality, freedom, emancipation and domination, the anticipation of death, and so on.

Certainly, within these historically sensitive currents (which were more deeply influenced by "Jerusalem" than "Athens," by the religious rather than the Greek, metaphysical heritage), I would further differentiate out the tradition of dialectical thinking. This line, reaching from Jakob Böhme through Oetinger and Schelling, Hegel and Marx up to Bloch, Benjamin, and, if you like, Foucault, contrasts with another, mystical line of thought beginning with Meister Eckhart and ending with Heidegger and perhaps Wittgenstein. While mystical contemplation is speechless, privileging a mode of intuition or recollection that repudiates the reasonableness of discursive thought, dialectical thought always criticizes the intellectual intuition, the intuitive access to the (supposedly) immediate. In the productive force of negation, dialectics recognizes its own proper impetus, the motor of a self-criticizing reason that Hegel celebrated as the rose in the cross of the present. In this tradition, philosophy takes seriously the problem of the Theologoumenon, of the God who assumes human form: the unconditioned character of moral obligation in the face of radical evil, the finitude of human freedom, the fallibility of spirit, and the mortality of the individual. Dialectics takes on the problem of theodicy, the suffering generated from the negativity of an inverted world. Such a world could never be experienced as something negative, as something inverted, were it to harden, so to say naturalistically, as the indifference of a merely contingent event. For example, I was already interested in Schelling's *On the Essence of Human Freedom* during my student years.

Mendieta   Many people, including yourself, have noted that the first Frankfurt School would not have been possible without Marx, but also not without Judaism. Many, if not most, of the first generation of the Frankfurt School were Jews. Their critique of society, in light of the Holocaust, could only be pronounced from the standpoint of a "damaged life," and the perpetual threat of barbarity and totalitarianism. Do you see yourself as inheriting, as standing in the stream of, this not so subterranean current, and if so, how?

Habermas   Well, Adorno himself understood his own critique of the reification of interpersonal relationships and intrapsychic energies as a consequence of the prohibition against images [*Bilderverbot*]. Reification is deification; the distortion of something conditioned into the Unconditioned. Negative-dialectical thought intends to rescue the non-identical in things, which otherwise are violated by our own abstractions. It attempts to reconstruct the integrity of those individuals who have been rendered dumb by an unavoidable subsumption. Adorno's work is guided by the intuition that a subjectivity run amok transforms everything around it into objects, elevating itself into an Absolute, and thereby running up against the true Absolute – against the unconditional right of each creature not to be overlooked, to be acknowledged for what it is. The rage of objectification ignores the essential core of the fully individuated Other, by which the creature is marked as having been made "in the image of God."

Looked at philosophically, the powerful cognitive impulse behind the "Axial Age" [*Achsenzeit*] is captured in the First Commandment, namely emancipation from the chain of lineage and from the arbitrary will of mythic powers. At that time the world religions, as they developed a monotheistic or acosmic concept of the Absolute, pierced through the uniform, flat surface of narratively interwoven, contingent appearance, thus tearing open the gap between deep and surface structure, between essence and appearance, which first granted humanity the freedom of reflection and the power to distance itself from the abyss of immediacy. With these concepts of the Absolute or the unconditioned, validity is distinguished from genesis, truth from health or soundness, guilt from causality, law from violence, and so forth. At that time, the constellation of concepts emerged which predetermine the problems that the philosophy of German Idealism would eventually face: the relation of the infinite to the finite, the unconditioned to the conditioned, unity to multiplicity, freedom to necessity.

Only after Hegel, with the Young Hegelians and Nietzsche, was this constellation taken up once again. But this "postmetaphysical" thought remained deeply ambiguous. To this day it remains threatened by the possibility of a relapse into "neopaganism." In the early 1930s, the Young Conservative precursors of fascism, under the inspiration of Hölderlin and Nietzsche, used this same term to describe their reclamation of the archaic sources of the Presocratics, of the "origins" *before* the sources of monotheism and the Platonic *logos*. In his posthumously published Spiegel interview, Heidegger still used this polytheistic jargon: "Only *a* god can save us . . ." As a consequence of the postmodernist critique of reason, these neopaganist intellectual figures have become fashionable again. Metaphors such as "networks," "family resemblances," "rhizomes," and so on may initially have the innocently pragmatic sense of sharpening our sensitivity for contexts. But in relation to Nietzsche's and Heidegger's critiques of metaphysics, they imply the rejection of the universalistic significance of unconditioned validity claims. Adorno was struggling against this regressive tendency within postmetaphysical thinking as he promised to keep faith with metaphysics "at the moment of its fall." Following Nietzsche, for him it was always a question of deepening the dialectical criticism of the "logic of essences," rather than the flat anti Platonism that circulates so thoughtlessly in today's modish late Heideggerian and late Wittgensteinian currents. In this intention, if not in the means of realizing it, I am in complete agreement with Adorno.

Mendieta   It is clear that the issues and points of departure for the second generation of the Frankfurt School were and remain different: the Cold War, the defense of democracy, the preservation and furthering of the hard won gains of the Enlightenment and modernity, the critique of new forms of reification and commodification, the discovery of the civilizing role of law, the overcoming of the philosophy of consciousness, etc. To what extent, however, has religion, in whatever form, truly ceased, if indeed it has, to inform the second generation's continuation of the Frankfurt School?

Habermas   I can't speak for the "second generation," but only for myself – or in what I say now perhaps also for Karl-Otto Apel.

I would not object to the claim that my conception of language and of communicative action oriented toward mutual understanding nourishes itself from the legacy of Christianity. The "telos of reaching understanding" – the concept of discursively directed agreement which measures itself against the standard of intersubjective recognition, that is, the double negation of criticizable validity claims – may well nourish itself from the heritage of a *logos* understood as Christian, one that is indeed embodied (and not just with the Quakers) in the communicative practice of the religious congregation. Already the communicative-theoretical version of the concept of emancipation in *Knowledge and Human Interests*[2] could be "unmasked" as the secularizing translation of the divine promise of salvation. (Of course, since then I have become more cautious when using the expression "emancipation" beyond the area of the biographical development of individual persons, since social collectives, groups, or communities cannot be imagined as subjects writ large.) I only want to say that the evidence of my relation to a theological heritage does not bother me, as long as one recognizes the *methodological difference* of the discourses; that is, as long as the philosophical discourse conforms to the distinctive demands of justificatory speech. In my view, a philosophy that oversteps the bounds of methodological atheism loses its philosophical seriousness.

Moreover, one doctrinal element of Jakob Böhme's mystical speculations on the "nature" that arises through an act of contraction, or the "dark ground" in God, has been of great significance for me. Later, Gershom Scholem called my attention to the counterpart of this element, Isaac Luria's doctrine of *zimzum*. Interestingly, these two independently developed speculations came together via Knorr von Rosenheim and Schwabian Pietism in the post-Fichtean idealism of Baader and Schelling. In the essay on the "Essence of Human Freedom" that I've already mentioned, and in his philosophy of the "Ages of the World," Schelling appropriated this tradition and anchored the tense relation between "egoity" and "love" in God Himself. The rather "dark" tendency toward finitization [*Verendlichung*] or contraction is intended as an explanation of God's capacity for self-limitation. This was the subject of my doctoral dissertation.

The problem concerns the creation of the *first* Adam, the decisive moment that brings the world-age of ideal creation – which, like the motion of Hegel's "logic," took place only within God's spirit – to its conclusion. In order to be able to see Himself confirmed in His own freedom through an alter ego, God must delimit himself precisely within this very freedom. That is, He equips Adam *kadmos* [first Adam] with the unconditional freedom of good and evil, and thus assumes the risk that Adam may make the wrong use of this gift by sinning and thereby dragging the whole of ideal creation with him into the abyss. He would thus topple God Himself from His throne. Of course, this "worst case scenario" is just what happened. The story solves the problem of theodicy, but at a tremendous cost: that first, horrific act of freedom inaugurates a new age of the world, the age of world history. In this second, historical age of the world, a humbled God must Himself await redemption, since humanity has taken on the burden of resurrecting fallen nature.

This myth – and it is more than just a myth – illuminates two aspects of human freedom: the *intersubjective constitution* of autonomy and the meaning of the *self-binding* of the will's arbitrary freedom to *unconditionally* valid norms.

Thus the creation of the first human yields an inevitable, catastrophic consequence. The act of creation already completed *in mente* must start all over again historically, from the very beginning, since no subject, not even God Himself, can be truly free without being recognized as free by at least one other subject – that is, by someone who is free *in the same sense* (and who, for his part, also requires such reciprocal recognition). No one can enjoy freedom alone, or at the cost of the freedom of another. Thus freedom may never be conceived merely negatively, as the absence of compulsion. Freedom conceived intersubjectively distinguishes itself from the arbitrary freedom of the isolated individual. No one is free until we all are free. This fact emphasizes the second aspect, the unconditioned character of moral obligation, insofar as the fate of God and the world as a whole stands in balance with the good and evil that historically acting subjects mutually attribute to one another. Humanity feels the weight of the categorical Ought in the superhuman responsibility for an inverse history of salvation. Inserted as authors into such a charged world history, they must answer to world history in the form of a last judgment implacably deferred into the future.

Mendieta Let me be more direct. In your essay "Reflections on a Remark of Max Horkheimer," you conclude, "it may perhaps be said that to seek to salvage an unconditional meaning without God is a futile undertaking, for it belongs to the peculiar dignity of philosophy to maintain adamantly that no validity claim can have cognitive import unless it is vindicated before the tribunal of justificatory discourse."[3] You wrote this in order to differentiate philosophy's particular type of unconditionality from religion's unconditionality, which offers consolation in light of suffering, defeat, and a misspent life. Philosophy's unconditionality is a quest for truth, and to this extent it is, or must be, postmetaphysical. Yet, somewhere else you write, "Philosophy, even in its postmetaphysical form, will be able neither to replace nor to repress religion as long as religious language is the bearer of a semantic content that is inspiring and even indispensable, for this content eludes (for the time being?) the explanatory force of philosophical language and continues to resist translation into reasoning discourses."[4] These two quotations are indicative of two conflicting tendencies in your work: in one tendency, religion is liquified and sublated in discourse ethics and the theory of communicative rationality; in the other, religion is given the function of preserving and even nurturing a particular type of "semantic" content that remains indispensable for ethics and morality, but also for philosophy in general.

Habermas   I see no contradiction there. In the discussion of Horkheimer I only wanted to show that the concept of an unconditioned truth can be defended not just with strong theological premises, but also under the more modest premises of postmetaphysical thinking. The second citation, on the other hand, expresses the conviction that indispensable potentials for meaning are preserved in religious language, potentials that philosophy has not yet fully exhausted, has not yet translated into the language of public, that is, of presumptively generally convincing, reasons. Taking the example of the concept of the individual person, which the religious language of monotheistic doctrine has indeed articulated from the very beginning with all the precision one could wish for, I have attempted to point out this deficit, or at least the clumsiness of philosophical attempts at translation. For me, the basic concepts of philosophical ethics, as they have developed up to this point, also fail to capture all the intuitions that have already found a more nuanced expression in the language of the Bible, and which we have only come to know by means of a halfway religious socialization. In light of this shortcoming, discourse ethics attempts a translation of the categorical imperative into a language that also lets us do justice to another intuition – I mean the feeling of "solidarity," the bond of a member of a community to her fellow members.

Mendieta We can return to this point. But let us remain with the second citation. You put the phrase "for the time being?" in parentheses. Is it your view that it is philosophy's goal to completely assimilate, to translate, to rework and to "sublate" all desirable religious content? Or do you expect that religion will forever resist all efforts at such an intervention – and that it thus always will remain unassimilable and inaccessible, and in a certain sense thus also autonomous and unavoidable?

Habermas I don't know. That will emerge if and when philosophy carries on its work on its religious heritage with more sensitivity than it has so far. I am not speaking of the neopagan project of a "work on myth" – this work has long since been carried out by religion and theology.

Mendieta The relationship between religion and theology is not unlike that between the lifeworld and philosophy. But just like the horizon of the lifeworld retreats at every advance made by philosophy, religion retreats as theology tries to capture the realms of religious experience. It seems to me that the divergent tendencies with respect to religion I have encountered in your work stem from a conflated reading of religion and theology.

Habermas I see what you are driving at. Theology would forfeit its identity if it attempted to detach itself from religion's dogmatic core – and with it from the religious language in which a religious community's practices of prayer, of confession, and of faith occur. These are the practices in which religious faith, which theology can only interpret, proves itself. From the beginning, theology has a certain parasitic or derivative status. It cannot hide the fact that its interpretive work can never entirely "recover" or "exhaust" the performative meaning of living faith. Now, you say: this is just as true for philosophy! Perhaps philosophy can "purloin" a few concepts from theology (as Benjamin put it in his "Theses on the Philosophy of

History"), but it would be the worst kind of intellectualism to expect that philosophy's "way of translation" could completely appropriate the forms of experience preserved in religious language.

In one sense this analogy limps, of course. Theology cannot provide a substitute for religion, for the latter's truth is nourished from the revealed Word, which from the beginning appears in religious not scholarly form. But philosophy has an entirely distinct relation to religion. It seeks to re-express what it learns from religion in a discourse that is independent of revealed truth. Thus, every philosophical translation, even Hegel's, inevitably loses the performative meaning of living faith. A philosophy that comes to depend on "destinies" [*Geschicke*], or take solace from them, is no philosophy at all. The ambition of philosophy's "translation program" is, if you like, to rescue the profane significance of interpersonal and existential experiences that have so far only been adequately articulated in religious language. In contemporary terms, I would think of responses to extreme situations of helplessness, loss of self, or the threat of annihilation, which "leave us speechless."

Mendieta   You have argued on numerous occasions that solidarity and justice are two sides of the same coin. More recently, you traced this idea to the very core of Christian religious experience.[5] But is not Christian solidarity based on the injunction to respect and take charge of the other beyond any law, any possibility of reciprocity, equality, retribution, or reward? God's complete otherness announces itself in the negativity of the suffering other. This other as divine epiphany commands and calls us beyond any calculation or triangulation. This is what one hears in the appellations of third world liberation theologians when they call for solidarity with the victims of both modernity and postmodernity. The preferential option for the poor seems to suggest that solidarity is prior to justice and thus more originary.

Habermas   Yes, the ethic of Christian love remains faithful to a devotion to the suffering other, an aspect that comes up short within an intersubjectively conceived morality of justice. Such a form of morality must limit itself to the grounding of commands that each will follow on the condition that they are also followed by every other. Of course, there is a good reason for this self-limitation. A supererogatory act, which transcends what can reasonably be expected of *everyone* on the basis of reciprocity, signifies the active sacrifice of one's own legitimate interests for the good, or the reduction of suffering of others in need of help. The imitation of Christ demands such a *sacrificium* from the faithful – on the condition, of course, that this active sacrifice, rendered holy in the light of a just and a Good God, an absolute Judge, is assumed freely. No earthly power may impose a sacrifice upon an autonomous will for supposedly higher ends. Thus the Enlightenment sought to abolish sacrifice. Today, this same skepticism is directed at the death penalty, as well as the legitimacy of a general obligation for military service. This is the basis of the careful, resigned limitation to a morality of justice. This certainly does not diminish our admiration for an absolute devotion to one's neighbor, nor does it reduce our respect, indeed our great admiration, for all those unspectacular, selfless sacrifices, mostly from mothers and women, without which the last moral bond would long ago have been broken in many pathologically distorted societies (and not just there).

Mendieta   Here, I would like to press you on this issue. At the same time, I would like to appeal to the type of criticisms made by people like Gutierrez, Boff, and Dussel. The standard of living of most people in the world is such that conditions of symmetry, reciprocity, reversibility, and so on are not only non-existent but almost unattainable. To these liberation theologians and philosophers a moral theory that stops at the abstract idea of the "moral point of view" is a luxury of the *state of exception* that the wealthy nations of the developed world enjoy. The status quo in most of the world, they say, is one of extreme privation and subhuman existence. Reciprocity will not do. We are called to do more than what is expected from a putative contract. Global responsibility today calls for action way above our mere call of duty. And this is what they mean by the "preferential option for the poor."

Habermas   I will leave aside for the moment the distinction between Kantianism and contractualism, and will also refrain from the objection that the criteria of a so-called "abstract justice," if only applied, would be entirely sufficient to revolutionize global society. Just imagine for a moment that the G-7 nations assumed global responsibility, and unified themselves through policies that met John Rawls' (contractualistically grounded) second principle of justice: "social and economic inequalities are to be arranged so that it is reasonably expected that they will bring the greatest advantage to the least well-off." The unjust distribution of good fortune in the world was certainly already a central concern of the great world religions. But in a secularized society, this problem primarily belongs on the political and economic table, not in the cupboard of morality, let alone of moral theory.

What is the scandal? In a world still dominated by nation-states, there is still no regime capable of the kind of political action that could assume the "global responsibility" demanded by moral points of view. And existing interest positions don't encourage the spontaneous formation of a political will that could implement a corresponding "moral division of labor" between the different members of an intolerably stratified world society. The burning issue of a just global economic order poses itself primarily as a political problem. How a democratically responsible politics can catch up with globalized markets that have outpaced it is, in any event, not a question for moral theory; social scientists and economists can contribute more to it than philosophers can. On the analytical level, it demands a great deal of empirical knowledge and institutional imagination. In the final analysis, of course, the best design is of no help unless the political process comes into play. On the practical level, only social movements will be able to create the necessary motivations beyond national borders.

The call of liberation theology, in its quest to lend a voice to the downtrodden, the oppressed, and the humiliated, does indeed stand within this context. I understand it as the active outrage against the inertia and the insensitivity of a status quo that no longer appears to move in the current of a self-accelerating modernization. The "more" of its brave, self-sacrificing engagement, extending far beyond all that could be reasonably expected, is justified by its participants through the Christian command of love. From another side, certainly, the supererogatory element of this personal intervention also appears as a reflex of powerlessness, though always an admirable one, in the face of the anonymous, systematic forces of politically untamed capitalism, which understand only the language of cost, not of morality.

Mendieta   As we close this century and millennium and attempt to take stock of what has transpired, one cannot help but agree with Hobsbawm: it was a century of extremes. But some might add: it was a century of "radical evil." There is something profoundly unforgivable and unassimilable in what transpired during the twentieth century. What can we have learned from the "radical evil" that we faced in this century?

Habermas The Holocaust was, up to the very moment it began, unimaginable; thus radical evil also has a historical index. What I mean is that there is a peculiar asymmetry in the knowledge of good and evil. We know what we may not do, what we must in each and every case refrain from doing, if we want to be able to look ourselves in the eye without blushing in shame. But we don't know what human beings as such are capable of. And the more evil increases, obviously, the stronger is the need to repress and forget those who have been wronged. This is the depressing experience of my own adult political life in the Federal Republic of Germany. But I have also had the good fortune of having another experience, which at least gives me hope that Richard Rorty is not entirely wrong when he, as an American, says what I would also express, though perhaps not with the same degree of self-confidence: "Nothing a nation has done should make it impossible for (citizens of) a constitutional democracy to regain self-respect."

Translated by Max Pensky

Notes

1 Jürgen Habermas, *The Postnational Constellation: Political Essays*, ed. and trans. Max Pensky (Cambridge: Polity, 2001).

2 Jürgen Habermas, *Knowledge and Human Interests*, trans. Jeremy J. Shapiro (Boston: Beacon Press, 1971).

3 "To Seek to Salvage an Unconditional Meaning without God is a Futile Undertaking: Reflections on a Remark of Max Horkheimer," in Jürgen Habermas, *Justification and Application: Remarks on Discourse Ethics*, trans. Ciaran Cronin (Cambridge: Polity, 1993), 146. See in this volume, page 108.

4 "Themes in Postmetaphysical Thinking" in Jürgen Habermas, *Postmetaphysical Thinking: Philosophical Essays*, trans. Fred Lawrence (Cambridge: Polity, 1992), 51.

5 See in particular Jürgen Habermas, *The Inclusion of the Other: Studies in Political Theory*, ed. and trans. Pablo DeGreiff and Ciaran Cronin (Cambridge: Polity, 1999), 10ff.

Index